VIOLENT
ECOTROPES

PHILIP AGHOGHOVWIA

Published by HSRC Press
Private Bag X9182, Cape Town, 8000, South Africa
www.hsrcpress.ac.za

First published 2022

ISBN (soft cover) 978-0-7969-2618-0
ISBN (pdf) 978-0-7969-2619-7

Copy-edited by Liz Sparg
Typeset by Richard Jones
Cover design by Nic Jooste
Cover photo by John Rourke on Unsplash
Printed by Kadimah Print, Cape Town, South Africa

Distributed in Africa by Blue Weaver
Tel: +27 (021) 701 4477; Fax Local: (021) 701 7302
www.blueweaver.co.za

Distributed in Europe and the United Kingdom by Eurospan Distribution Services (EDS)
Tel: +44 (0) 17 6760 4972; Fax: +44 (0) 17 6760 1640
www.eurospanbookstore.com

Distributed in the US, its possessions, Canada, and Asia by Lynne Rienner Publishers, Inc.
Tel: +1 303-444-6684; Fax: +1 303-444-0824; Email: cservice@rienner.com
www.rienner.com

Suggested citation: Philip Aghoghovwia (2022) *Violent Ecotropes: Petroculture in the Niger Delta*.
Cape Town: HSRC Press

For Makhosazana, Kesiena and Ebru

– my loves and believers in the truest sense!

Contents

Acknowledgements

This book has benefitted from interminable conversations with several interlocutors, colleagues and mentors to whom I owe a world of debt I certainly cannot repay. Major sections of this book – some parts reframed, some repeated verbatim – are the product of my doctoral thesis completed under the capable guidance of Louise Green and Nwabisa Bangeni at Stellenbosch University. Their insistence that profundity is the culmination of lucid writing remains a guiding objective towards which I aspire. If I have come up short here, it is only an indication of the "incompleteness" of every intellectual work.

I gratefully acknowledge the permission to include material that appeared in print in earlier versions elsewhere: parts of the prologue appeared in *Fueling Culture: 101 Words for Energy and Environment* (Fordham UP, 2017, pp. 238–241), edited by Imre Szeman and Jennifer Wenzel; parts of Chapter 1 on the work of Nnimmo Bassey appeared in *English in Africa* 41, no. 2 (2014): 59–77, and in *Handmaiden of Death: Apocalypse and Revelation* (Brill, 2016, pp. 85–95); parts of Chapter 3 appeared in *Alternation*, Special Issue 6 (2013): 175–196, and in *Social Dynamics* 43, no. 1 (2017): 32–45; parts of the Epilogue appeared in *Climate Realism: The Aesthetics of Weather and Atmosphere in the Anthropocene* (Routledge, 2020, pp. 33–46), edited by Lynn Badia, Marija Cetinic and Jeff Diamanti. I thank the Taylor and Francis Group for their kind permission to reproduce some of these works here. I appreciate the efforts of the editorial and production team at HSRC Press in bringing this book to fruition. I wish to thank the two anonymous reviewers for their attentive reading of my work and for their thoughtful suggestions. All omissions, infelicities and opinions in this book are my responsibility.

At Rhodes University where I worked briefly as a postdoctoral fellow, Dan Wylie was a gracious host and mentor whose stellar work in ecocriticism inspired my thinking; Dirk Klopper and Lynda Spencer opened their home, their arms and their hearts to me, ensuring that I wanted for nothing; Nelson Odume has remained a brother in the truest sense ever since.

At the University of Cape Town where I was a University Research Council postdoctoral fellow, Meg Samuelson took me under her intellectual wing. Meg's intellectual rigour and generosity in mentorship are a beacon that continues to light up my path. Lesley Green and Hedley Twidle provided an intellectual home for me at the Environmental Humanities South programme. The postgraduate workshops and seminars in which I participated and sometimes taught, and the stimulating conversations generated from them, shaped the thinking that went into this book. Harry Garuba inspired my development in a variety of ways. No other loss to death has affected me as has the passing of Harry, since my own dad passing 20 years ago.

Harry was my teacher, mentor and friend. He taught me as if I were his son, he mentored me as if I were his peer, and he befriended me as if I were his mate. Harry left me with a blueprint of how to be genuine and, in the process, free! And freely did he live and love until he left us that February morning.

At the West Africa Research Center, Dakar, Senegal, where I spent a few months writing, Ousmane Sene, Marianne Yade and several colleagues went beyond duty to ensure that I had a fruitful and memorable stay.

Onookome Okome has been a dear mentor and friend for many years. The COVID-19 pandemic prevented me from taking up the research residency at the University of Alberta, Canada, which he had helped to facilitate in early 2020.

For the collegial atmosphere in which to work and think at the University of the Free State's English Department, my thanks go to Susan Brokensha, Mariza Brooks, Thinus Conradie, Rick de Villiers, Colleen du Plessis, Carla Els, Hanta Henning, Stacey Khojane, Iri Manase, Karen McGuire and Helene Strauss.

I have been sustained by the friendship and encouragement of numerous friends in a variety of ways. Thanks to Aghogho Akpome, Stephen David, Michael Efeakpor, Esthie Hugo, Cajetan Iheka, Kimani Kaigai, Robert Muponde, Ogaga Okuyade, Senayon Olaoluwa, Riaan Oppelt, Ochuko Oputu, Poly and Chika Orji, Uhuru Phalafala, Byron Santangelo, Helene Strauss and Jennifer Wenzel.

This work has benefitted from generous grants from the African Humanities Program (AHP) of the American Council of Learned Societies (ACLS) funded by the Carnegie Corporation of New York; the National Research Foundation (NRF) of South Africa; the Research Office and the Transformation of the Professoriate Programme (2020–2022) of the University of the Free State, especially Henriette van den Berg, Eleanor van der Westhuizen and Riana Visser. Thanks to Andrzej Tymowski and Katie Smith. I am appreciative of the support and mentorship of the Department of Higher Education and Training (DHET) Future Professoriate Programme (FPP) under the leadership of Jonathan Jansen, Jackie du Toit and Neil Roos.

For their love, companionship and sustenance, eternal debt is owed to Makhosazana, Kesiena and Ebru, dedicatees of this book and the nucleus of my world.

Prologue

To write about the violence and culture of oil extraction is to write about the Niger Delta, the very theatre of energy production. Indeed, one cannot write about energy culture in the context of postcolonial Niger Delta without engaging the spectacle of violence it elicits, both in the public mind and in the sphere of creative imagination. This is precisely because of the form of sociality that oil energy generates in the cultural production of this region: it scripts in idioms of violence. My concern is less with the destructiveness the violence inflicts (which is considerable) than with the intricacies of its operation in the Niger Delta, especially the affect and spectacle that characterise its coexistence alongside oil.

In 2012, I attended an exhibition, *Delta Remix: Last Rites Niger Delta*, which displayed images related to the post-Saro-Wiwa era of oil production in Nigeria. It was a "representational intervention" of "remixed" images from a catalogue commissioned and published by the Goethe-Institut, with the title *Last Rites Niger Delta: The Drama of Oil Production in Contemporary Photographs*.[1] The photographs in the catalogue capture the violence that oil production perpetuates in the Delta, both on the landscape and in the life of the population.[2] The title of the book merits reflection. "Last rites" evokes a sense of ritual and ceremony, and a loaded eschatological undertone surrounds this rite of transition that precedes death. "Last Rites Niger Delta" projects a certain presence and performance of violence in the Niger Delta, self-inflicted by acts of community protest and visited upon the ecosphere by the technologies and politics of oil extraction.

The exhibition I attended attempted to capture the everyday realities of oil production and its manifest social and environmental repercussions in the Niger Delta. It provoked robust debates at the Johannesburg Workshop on Theory and Criticism around questions of environmental devastation, militancy by local communities as a means of protesting perceived injustice, and, finally, the vexing question of representation. What protocols of representation are available for negotiating and understanding the oil energy cultures in Nigeria?

In the Nigerian setting, as elsewhere, "representation" is a controversial term because it defies a clearly delineated epistemology. Perhaps this explains why Judith Butler recognises representation as an "operative term within a political process that seeks to extend visibility and legitimacy".[3] Indeed, visibility and legitimacy are interlinked and brought into sharp focus in the Niger Delta context; yet the relationship between them is fraught, as is evident in the text, *Last Rites*. In the Niger Delta, claims to legitimacy are at odds with the modality of violence through which they are made visible.

Violence is a crucial yet complex trope in Nigeria's energy culture. In the Delta it takes multiple, intricately related forms and textures that are both spectacular and subtle. In its subtle form, violence is, as Rob Nixon argues, slow and deficient in visibility.[4] Slow violence permeates every aspect of oil production in Nigeria, which complicates the understanding of any specific instance of violence. The situation of oil extraction in the Niger Delta obstructs and destabilises the idiom in which violence is articulated. In figures 1 and 2, I examine two photographs from the exhibition in terms of these dynamics, paying particular attention to how legitimacy or claims to legitimacy coalesce with insurrectionary visibility and thereby complicate the forms of violence that operate in Nigeria's cultural landscape.

Figure 1 *The first oil wellhead, also known as "Christmas Tree" (Kadir van Lohuizen,* Last Rites Niger Delta, *p. 21)*

Figure 1 depicts the signpost that marks the first oil well in the Niger Delta, yet the image lacks any sense of historical monumentality. On the timeworn, rusted sign is written "Oloibiri Well No. 1. Drilled June, 1956. Depth: 12,000 Feet". The signboard is in a sorry state, the fast-fading inscriptions on its rusty white board increasingly less visible amidst the encroaching bush. Yet, this neglected signboard is, in fact, symptomatic of the invisibility of Oloibiri – and perhaps the entire Niger Delta – on Nigeria's social development agenda, despite this village bearing the first fruits of commercial oil production for the Nigerian state. A cursory look at the photograph reveals, along the lines of Butler's analysis of the operations of representation, how both legitimacy and visibility are entangled and at work in this site.

Figure 2: *Macon Hawkins, an American oil worker held hostage by the Movement for the Emancipation of the Niger Delta (MEND) (Michael Kamber,* Last Rites Niger Delta, *p. 11)*

Figure 2 was released to the press by the insurgent group Movement for the Emancipation of the Niger Delta (MEND), as part of their guerrilla propaganda, in February 2006. This photograph has since gone viral on the Internet, and it has been read as an iconic image of militarised sociality of energy production and the spectacular violence that flourishes in the Niger Delta. In a broader context, this image can be read in terms of conventions of representation that depict Africa as a crisis-ridden outback of filth, poverty, sickness, violence, insurgents, war and death. Indeed, the Niger Delta embodies all of these; however, why is there this obsession with such dramatic images of youth violence, which Michael Watts describes as "the masked militant armed with the ubiquitous Kalashnikov, the typewriter of the illiterate"?[5] What currently remains of this quintessential image of the spectacle of violence that the oil complex in the Niger Delta seems to elicit in the public mind? Looking carefully at the photograph itself, one can observe the exaggerated staging of violence, the overly posed stance of the man holding the bazooka against the head of the white man at a proximity so ludicrous, it puts the captor in as much danger as his captive. This speaks volumes about violence for publicity that global media networks enable.

How is one to understand MEND's release of this image, in terms of the relationship between their claims to legitimacy and the hypervisibility of violence the photograph evokes and its correlate circulation and reception? What the viral circulation of the photograph has produced is the valorisation of violence through the reification of a militarised image, which works to undercut and demonise those claims to legitimacy that revolutionary politics might catalyse. How does one raise awareness about the injustices of oil extraction in local communities, and at the same time "challenge the privileging of the visible" that distorts?[6]

In attempting to draw attention to their social and environmental plights through propaganda and guerrilla tactics, the "militants" complicate their claims to legitimacy by falling into the trap of violence in its intricate operation – a violence that constitutes for itself and within itself "the news", an ideological operation that, as Edward Said notes, "determine[s] the political reality" of a phenomenon.[7] The workings of such operations contaminate the youth's moral claims for justice as they are made visible through the instrumentality of representation.

The political reality of cultural expression in the Niger Delta, which seeks to make visible the felt experience of petro-injustice, stages violence as a form of performance. This performance of violence is the visible expression of the experience of violence that is felt but that eludes visibility because of the nature of its operation in the Niger Delta. In any case, what is salient is that the slow violence of environmental injustice is further elided by the spectacle that characterises the manner of its representation, by which it is protested and made visible. Indeed, this spectacle tends to become the violence in itself. The spectacle of militancy, of gun-toting youths wearing army fatigues, on motorised boats, has come to constitute itself in the public mind as the characteristic violence of the Niger Delta, especially given the dominance of militarised insurgency in Nigeria's petromodernity.

Introduction

> We must understand that oil is not just a patrimony. It is something that
> is woven around the identity of the people. It gives a certain measure
> of control of the resources they have, that they have control over the
> environment they live in; this all enhances their sense of identity.[8]

The condition of violence that proliferates in the oil landscape of the Niger Delta is an appropriate opening for this book, which investigates the relationship between cultural production, oil extraction and the environment in a postcolonial context of Nigeria's Niger Delta. The book seeks to understand the ways in which environmental concerns and representations of oil are captured in literary and other cultural forms, and how these imaginings enable an understanding of the social world of the Niger Delta. The materials assembled for analysis, which include poetry, film and photographs, perform certain affirmative politics. They represent in less spectacular ways than the photographs discussed in the preface; but together they depict various strands of the experience of inhabiting the sites and embodying the social contradictions and environmental repercussions of oil extraction in the Niger Delta.

The book takes as its frame of reference the post-Saro-Wiwa era in Niger Delta. The significance of the environmental rights activist Ken Saro-Wiwa to this project is in the geopolitical and ethical contestations that his activist life and political polemics perform in the context of the Niger Delta struggle. The book focuses on works produced after his extrajudicial murder in 1995. I enlist several works, produced between 1998 and 2015, to advance the notion that literary and cultural production, in a post-Saro-Wiwa context, apprehend certain moments of catharsis in Nigeria's chequered postcolonial history. This is a time when the trajectories of the oil encounter have tended to invoke and imaginatively realise Paul Anderson's 2007 film adaptation with that disturbing and evocative title: *There Will Be Blood* – wherever crude oil is extracted.[9] Indeed, the literary figurations studied in this book suggest that there is catastrophe – human, material and environmental – operating alongside the production of oil in the Niger Delta.

Saro-Wiwa was a writer and an environmental rights activist. He was at once an inspiring and a controversial figure in postcolonial Nigeria. He is remembered as a politician, successful businessperson, newspaper columnist, television scriptwriter and producer, and prolific creative writer. His detractors demonise him for his role in the Nigeria/Biafra Civil War of 1967–1970, as he was said to have supported the Nigerian state against the secessionist Biafra – for which he was rewarded with the position of Civilian (Sole) Administrator of Bonny Council in the eastern delta.[10] He is perceived to have benefitted not only from the Civil War (which was in part fought over access to and control over crucial oil fields) but also from the fraught geopolitics of Nigeria's federalism that he would later campaign against in the 1990s. To the international community and his admirers within Nigeria, he was a champion of environmental rights and social justice, especially for the Ogoni and other minority peoples around the world. His campaigns against environmental pollution and the decimation of the agricultural economy of the Ogoni People, in which the Nigerian government and Shell Oil Corporation were complicit, attracted international attention; one example was his success in framing the Ogoni agitations within the project of Unrepresented Nations and Peoples Organisation (UNPO), The Hague.

In May 1994, four Ogoni chiefs and senior members of the Movement for the Survival of the Ogoni Peoples (MOSOP) were lynched to death by a mob of protesters after being accused of betraying their community to the federal government and compromising their principles for selfish gains. The mobsters who committed this atrocity were alleged to be members of the youth assemblage of MOSOP who were loyal to Saro-Wiwa, the then spokesperson for MOSOP. He and eight other leaders were arrested and blamed for the killing of the elders. Having consistently staged non-violent international campaigns on the atrocities oil extraction was bringing to Ogoniland, to embarrass the Nigerian government and the oil corporations, Saro-Wiwa was no doubt marked for destruction by the Nigerian military junta and, perhaps, Big Oil (especially Shell). He was perceived as a powerful threat because of his international recognition as a writer and activist, and more concerning, for stirring up international sentiments against Big Oil's affairs in the Niger Delta. The charge of complicity in the murder of the four Ogoni elders, though unsubstantiated, was just the pretext his adversaries needed to silence him. Therefore, this accusation of murder provided the Sani Abacha junta with an opportune pretext to accomplish their plan and drive Saro-Wiwa's organisation underground.

On 10 November 1995, Saro-Wiwa and eight others – Barinem Kiobel, John Kpunien, Baribor Bera, Saturday Dobee, Felix Nwate, Nordu Eawo, Paul Levura and Daniel Gbokoo – were executed for inciting youth to murder the four Ogoni elders. His death produced an effect that was antithetical to that intended by his accusers. The ripple effect marked the beginning of a new and more radical form of representation of the ecological repercussions on the Niger Delta landscape. It brought to the fore a robust and intensely embattled opposition to the oil extraction industry, and its repercussions on the Niger Delta ecology. It also inflamed international opprobrium against Abacha's dictatorship in Nigeria. This led to international sanctions and the expulsion of Nigeria from the Commonwealth Group of Nations in 1995. Saro-Wiwa's murder by state executive decree has also been a sort of moral albatross that dented the corporate image of Shell Petroleum Development Company in the eyes of the global community. It is not out of magnanimity, for instance, that Shell agreed to pay USD15.5 million to the family of Saro-Wiwa and the Ogoni Eight, as part of an out-of-court settlement for their role in the murder of the Ogoni leaders and environmental rights activists.[11]

Critics Chinyere Nwahunanya and Godini Darah argue that the Niger Delta not only hosts Nigeria's economic hub, crude oil, but also its literary creativity. As

Nwahunanya notes, "it is often not recognised that while the Niger Delta has made tremendous and inestimable contributions to the Nigerian economy, it has also literally championed the evolution and sustenance of Nigerian literature by the fact of its contribution to the intellectual bank through creative literature.[12] Darah, on the other hand, traces literary creativity in the Niger Delta to its earliest precolonial tradition of an exchange of letters through coastal trade and cultural bilateral relationships with precolonial/pre-slave Europe. Darah concludes that "the flourish of literary works by both old and young Niger Delta writers [makes] the region… the most active site of literary creativity in Nigeria".[13] American postcolonial critic Jennifer Wenzel further extends this connection in *The Disposition of Nature: Environmental Crisis and World Literature* (2020), noting the imbrication of oil and literary production in the birthing and unravelling of Nigeria as a nation state.[14] Wenzel surmises that rather than fuelling the imagination of the nation into fashioning a modern democratic nation state with the oil wealth it generates, "oil hijacks the imagination…promising wealth without work and progress without the passage of time".[15] The result, she argues, following the work of such thinkers as Benedict Anderson, Fernando Coronil, Ryszard Kapuscinski and Andrew Apter, is "the *unimagining* of the Niger Delta",[16] in terms of both the ecological disaster that follows the trajectory of oil extraction and the geopolitical marginalisation that the region suffers in the hands of the nation state.

In identifying and building on their points, this book is located in a post-Saro-Wiwa literary and cultural context, exploring writings produced between 1998 and 2015. Nevertheless, I am interested in how Saro-Wiwa's polemical writing, political life and, ultimately, his death, provide a somewhat grand narrative of geopolitical and cultural resistance to the social and environmental repercussions of oil extraction. The political contradictions and ecological injustice that provoked Saro-Wiwa's global campaigns continue to shape the literary and cultural expression emanating from this region. In the representation of the social world of the Niger Delta, conceptions of the human subject acquire a new meaning, especially in relation to petro-ecology and the postcolonial state of Nigeria. If, as Darah argues, "literature has become an extension of the politics of emancipation and human rights",[17] then "Saro-Wiwa's ghost" has tended to loom large in the cultural imagination of oil extraction in the Niger Delta. In modelling literary creativity on Saro-Wiwa, to address questions of ecological injustice in the Niger Delta, recent writers deploy their arts, as Nwahunanya suggests, to "put literature in the service of society by allowing it to perform a political and cultural function".[18] Moreover, Saro-Wiwa's heroic qualities have also gained salience in the moral and political aesthetics around which films are scripted in the Nigerian movie industry, known as Nollywood. In the video films produced around the subject of oil and its environmental impacts, especially in the revolutionary textures of insurgency and violence in the Niger Delta, Saro-Wiwa looms large in the manner in which narratives are spawned.[19] Nollywood returns to the intellectual, legendary, activist figure of Saro-Wiwa to create stock characters modelled on his archetype, as a way of not only propagating his legacy but also inflecting the crucially pertinent discourse of environmentalism, to which the films bear witness and which they contextually re-enact for public consumption and debate.[20]

The Niger Delta is the quintessential theatre of oil extraction in Africa. A landscape of profound paradox, this bioregion brims with prodigious oil reserves and overwhelming social and ecological deprivations. It is a situation that stimulates much intellectual interest, and at the same time fashions a culture of militancy whose politics of resistance exacerbates the issues it purports to address. In short, this site of oil extraction is a theatre of violence. It represents in the public imagination the extremely negative effects of oil extraction on the environment, provoking community protests and youth violence as ways of drawing attention to the problem. In turn, the upheavals in the region have produced a body of literary and cultural expression that depicts and magnifies the local voices of protest against extraction. Previous studies, especially in social anthropology and political science, have focused on the petro-related violence in the region, presenting it as a materially based response to the failure of governance and environmental pollution.[21] In literary studies, scholars have examined this failure in the broader cultural context of Nigeria's faltering nationhood, focusing on the poetics of otherness and marginalisation as the loci from which to apprehend the oil encounter.[22]

However, to analyse political-economic crises of oil extraction in terms of otherness and marginalisation seems insufficient, because violence also features as a metonymic device employed in representations of the oil ontology, the lived reality in the environments of extraction. That is to say that violence names the various forms of intrusion and disruption, which literary and cultural representation describes as part of everyday experience in the oil sites. By moving from the poetics of otherness or marginalisation to naming representations of the oil ontology as violence that limns more than physical acts of confrontation, this book offers more generative insights that pull towards broader forces beyond the ken of local (national) politics that attends oil extraction in the Niger Delta.

This book proposes a new interpretation of the culture of oil extraction in three broad interventions: (1) it rethinks the domain of representation, in terms of the imaginative possibilities that frame attempts at representing oil in culture; (2) it reconceptualises place regarding the complexities of engaging the globalised infrastructure of fossil fuel extraction from the specificity of local, indigenous lived ecologies; and (3) it reframes the environmental challenges that carbon-based civilisation poses to local landscapes as concrete instances of anthropogenic global warming, without getting lost in the globalising logic and abstracting scientism that frame climate change discourse. I argue in this book that together these constitute significant factors that shape and are shaped by oil energy and the global circuits within which it travels to feed international consumption.

The first node of this book's intervention discusses representation itself, the means by which "the story of oil" gets told. The attempt here is to pose questions about the imaginative possibilities that might adequately frame and signify the oil encounter in the Niger Delta, in all its valences. The Indian writer Amitav Ghosh popularises the phrase "the oil encounter", writing about the absence of a truly great literary form that can adequately capture the magnitude of the oil ontology in literature. In "Petrofiction: The Oil Encounter and the Novel" (1992),[23] Ghosh suggests that there is little presence of oil in cultural expression and reflects on why the "oil encounter has proved so imaginatively sterile".[24] He argues that representing something of such magnitude as the oil encounter can only be done adequately in literature through narratives of epic quality or of significant historical depth and intellectual seriousness. He claims that this absence of a truly satisfactory literary expression of oil has made the oil encounter suffer a representational crisis,[25] not only in the American literary circuit but also, and even more so, in other worlds where oil is extracted, namely the Middle East, Africa and South America.[26] Yet, when we consider the Niger Delta, literary representation explores particular historical contexts – geopolitical and environmental – that constellate around the production of oil and the petromodernity it brings into being.

This book brings these concatenating forms of relations into relief, showing how literary and cultural representations engage the oil encounter, both its form and its subject matter, within a framework of critical realism. Given the interminable political debates and environmental discourses that surround oil extraction in the Niger Delta, depictions of the oil encounter are juxtaposed with the material textures of the everyday. Therefore, as I argue throughout the book, representation of the oil encounter is marked by a transgressive impulse to inflect realism and, by extension, reality, to better articulate the overwhelming experience of the various forms of violence of extraction in the local environment. In other words, I argue that conventional realism does not serve the purpose of their representational advocacy. Rather, what confronts the fictive possibility is an experience of the real, so steeped in deprivations it becomes almost unreal, dreamlike, overwhelming the narrative schema that results in fragmentations, narrative incoherence and contradictions in point of view, as these figure in the representation.

The second dimension to this book's intervention is the conception of place. The end of the Cold War saw capital (and capitalism) shake off whatever restraints that might have kept it in check. National borders collapsed to allow unbridled and unmitigated neoliberalism to take root, accessing natural resources wherever they may be located. Oil (or more generally, fossil fuel) is the quintessential global commodity that operates within this neoliberal logic of free market borderless-ness. Its extraction exemplifies the untrammelled hemispheric reach of capital; it is not subject to nor is it conditioned by state regulations.[27] The landscapes of oil production are considered intrinsically displaced, heterogeneous and international. James Ferguson considers it an insular and socially thin neoliberal landscape of deregulated enterprises.[28] Indeed, oil gorges out of its hosting locality an internationally constituted infrastructure and circuits of flow to feed global consumption. This book complicates this internationalist character of oil extraction, showing how literary practice goes against this form of globalism; it issues from a clearly defined sense of place, autochthonous and vernacular, which is at odds with the internationalist logic of oil's global industrial complex. As will become clear throughout the book, by place is meant the interaction that a landscape shares with the lifeworld that inhabits it, consisting of objects, entities, people, plants, animals and natural resources. Place is not just a space from which certain provincial or local identities coalesce and assert against perceived infractions, it is also an ecology marked by habitability: a capacity to inhabit life, all forms of life.[29] Part of what this book does, therefore, is to theorise the literary and cultural imagination of the Niger Delta as an articulation of a place-based, place-specific form of petroculture. I turn attention to the way in which literary depiction engages the Niger Delta as a bastion of globalism. This globalism is produced as functioning within an insidious circuit of non-being for the locals, even when all forms of life in the local environment are intimately intertwined with extraction. Moreover, stating it in this way, this book looks beyond the "oil curse" characterisation, a phrase usually associated with the discourse of oil, its extraction and governance in Nigeria in some of the work done in studies on oil, culture and politics.[30] By contrast, the book is located in recent studies in energy humanities, following the example of such thinkers as Stephanie LeMenager. LeMenager is interested in the ways that literary and cultural depictions of place, like the oilscape of the Niger Delta, attend to "what persists in the face of oil – life, culture"[31] and the will to survive oil's detritus on the local environment. Indeed, the question of place in thinking about environment in the Niger Delta is borne out of the need to give voice to "silenced or marginalised perspectives as situated in particular communities",[32] and to resist certain logic that pretends to be universal but that only serves narrow interests.

This impulse to resist an universalising discourse of the global climate crisis – and of oil's extractivism, which partly exacerbates it – is taken further in the third and final intervention that this book makes. Apprehending the environmental challenges that oil extraction poses to local habitats within the globalised discourse of climate change is a difficult task. Prevailing iterations of the Anthropocene, that is, human actions as vectors driving climate change, tend to elide the specificities of site-based, local events of climate change, presenting human-induced changes of the earth's climate in abstract terms by means of scientific modelling and speculative projections. This process of articulating the climate crisis glosses over the particularity of local and provincial experiences.

The term "Anthropocene" is credited to the Nobel-winning chemist Paul Crutzen and former biologist Eugene Stoermer. According to Crutzen and Stoermer,[33] "Anthropocene" tentatively names the current epoch of the earth's ecology in a time when an otherwise infinitesimal human history, within the broader natural history of the earth, has become an agential character, a "dramatis personae" and scripter of the "geostory" of our blue planet.[34] Crutzen and Stoermer enumerate how human activities on the planet in the last two centuries have accelerated the changes in the earth's climate, beginning, for instance, with James Watts's invention of the steam engine in 1784. Crutzen and Stoermer consider the impact of humankind on the earth's ecology as constituting "a significant geological, morphological force" proportionate to an event of nature that brought about other geological epochs or time scales, such as the Holocene, which has lasted for eleven thousand years.[35] Hence, the authors coined a new term, "Anthropocene", which denotes the anthropogenic character of the current climate change.

There have been intense debates regarding the various implications of this coinage,[36] one being about the date that best marks the onset of the Anthropocene.[37] In 2017 the World Geological Society agreed on the date of 1945, set from around the end of World War II, because it marked the beginning of the Great Acceleration, the explosion of the atom bombs, and the intensification of nuclear activities by the competing superpowers of the twentieth century.[38] Still, no concrete agreement has been reached on the extant implications of the term; no one has yet had the final word. In short, the term "Anthropocene" has raised more questions than answers, and some critics have begun to call the coinage into question. Eileen Crist, for example, questions the "narcissistic overtones" that the "naming of an epoch after ourselves" carries,[39] noting that such a gesture is self-reflexively "anthropocentric" and mutually co-extensive with the "worldview that generated the Anthropocene… in the first place".[40] Other thinkers would even like to see a framework that situates the anthropogenic effects of the earth's ecology within a critique of capitalism. Jason Moore's edited collection is an important intervention in that regard.[41] Similarly, Naomi Klein, in her bestselling book *This Changes Everything* (2015), suggests the climate crisis is attendant on the prevailing political economy of capitalism and therefore a human problem that needs an equally human solution, but that "we have not done the things that are necessary to lower carbon emissions because those things fundamentally conflict with deregulated capitalism".[42] Klein surmises that the climate crisis is "a battle between capitalism and the planet".[43] Thus, any genuine attempt to address the problem would have to confront head-on the prevailing political economy of capitalism. Dipesh Chakrabarty presents a somewhat different view, suggesting that a critique of capital in and of itself is "insufficient to account" for the processes of the earth's changes, as these require "geological and paleoclimatological knowledge" in addition.[44] He notes that what specialists need to reflect on, however, is the "uneven responsibility" the term "Anthropocene" places on the generic term "man" – "Anthropos" being attributed with a geological force, a fact, he notes, that needs to be addressed within a framework of justice.[45]

The interminable wrangling over the Anthropocene concept is attendant on its unevenness[46] and its universalising tendency. This universalising discourse of the Anthropocene ramifies in at least two ways. First is the entity "humanity" – or "Anthropos" – around which (or more precisely, around whom) the Anthropocene discourse is organised. It is a term much despised, noted Chakrabarty, because of its unresolved historical baggage and "ideological trappings".[47] The central thesis of the Anthropocene suggests that human activity is fundamentally altering and hastening the earth's climate and weather patterns. The implication of this notion is that all of humanity is to blame for the voracious exploitation of the earth's resources.

The science and politics of global warming identify *collective humanity* – as the term "Anthropocene" suggests – as a geological force driving the earth's ecology and rewriting its natural history. This otherwise convincing discourse presents humanity as if, historically, that label has always meant a unified constituency of human beings; as if humanity was not, until only recently, bifurcated between what Jean-Paul Sartre describes as "men" and "natives".[48] Indeed, "Homo sapiens may constitute a singular actor [in the Anthropocene]…but it is not a unitary one".[49] What the science and politics of global warming have not sufficiently accounted for is that the "humans" it refers to are just a few concentrated in one small disproportionately rich part of the world. These humans, who consist of less than 20 per cent of the world's population or "one-fifth of humanity"[50] are citizens of the industrialised nations whose rapid development was driven by the easily accessible and abundant supply of carbon-based energy. The citizens of these industrialised nations, as Timothy Mitchell notes, have developed unsustainable lifestyles and profligate cultures, consuming 80 per cent of the earth's resources, and in the process putting "carbon that was previously stored underground" in the atmosphere, "where it is causing increases in global temperatures" and putting great strains on the earth's capacity to recalibrate itself.[51]

The second ramification of the prevailing iterations of the Anthropocene is its tendency to elide the specificities of site-based, local events of the earth's changes. The changes in the earth's climate are presented as characterised by unusual, volatile weather patterns, often abstracted and charted by means of scientific modelling, the devastating effects palpable and also imminent, dire consequences which could still be staved off and possibly "reversed to the Holocene-like stage" if certain steps are taken.[52] While embedding and engaging this global discourse, this book reflects on the Anthropocene as a profound actuality of place. The landscape of the Niger Delta provides evidence of devastations of apocalyptic proportions that render all scientific projections anachronistic; the apocalyptic future projected as a possible or imminent occurrence is already a quotidian reality in this petroleumscape. This book therefore brings the specific discursive textures of provincial environments of the Niger Delta into the fray. I consider how the body of literary and cultural texts studied in this book inaugurate a transnational discourse of environmentalism in a manner that extends ecocriticism. More specifically, the transnational dialogue initiated by this body of work on the Niger Delta in part enriches contemporary global debates on climate change by infusing the abstracting discourse with the actuality of real events that are happening in apocalyptic proportions. I argue that the representation of oil extraction's impact on the locality reframes the climate change discourse – not as abstract processes captured and charted by means of scientific modelling, but rather, as actual lived events happening in real time: oil spills and blowouts, which pollute water bodies; the visible oil sludge rendering vast farmlands and coastal plains wastelands; gas flares that light up the skies and deny surrounding communities the respite of twilight. Literary apocalypticism therefore vivifies environmental challenges of our time by mobilising metaphor to frame global climate change as a profound actuality of place.

Postcolonial ecocriticism, the Niger Delta and petro-environmentalism

The field of postcolonial ecocriticism has been slow to develop, precisely because ecocriticism and postcolonial studies have often run the risk of talking *past* rather than *to* each other.[53] For instance, previously colonised peoples and their environments constantly confront the quandary of negotiating between ecological wellbeing and the seductions of economic exigencies, ones that purport to advance desperately needed developments but that are often antithetical to local existence and to quotidian life. Nevertheless, the important studies done by postcolonial scholars in the last decade bring these concerns into conversation under the rubric of postcolonial ecocriticism, foregrounding areas of important convergence.[54] The strong version of these critics' arguments is that both disciplines are mutually coextensive and thus unified in their critique against human hubris, evident mostly in imperialism and anthropocentric modernity, two of the most impactful vectors that index human activity and its footprint on the earth. More specifically, Euro-American imperialism and its attendant capitalist modernity have exacted much violence on the environment and peoples of the colonised world, whose resources have fed the engines of contemporary consumer capitalism. The form of globalism that this combination unleashes registers the impulse to extract from the people and environments deemed inferior or inconsequential to the ontological constitution of imperialism (read Euro-American) as the universalising, and therefore normative, condition of being. Thus, postcolonial ecocriticism in Africa is largely a critique of the combination of modernisation, globalisation and capitalism (including the collusion of some crass African leadership), which have opened African peoples and environments to rampant exploitation and trauma.

Nixon, in *Slow Violence and the Environmentalism of the Poor* (2011), provides an innovative way of conceiving these issues under the ken of postcolonial ecocriticism. The concept of "structural violence", he argues, does not adequately describe the insidious and often invisible effects of environmental degradation of local, provincial environments that often take place over the *longue durée*. Nixon provides useful insights for understanding environmental pollution and the inequitable distribution of a country's resources as another form of violence: a non-physical violence, inflicted incrementally, both directly and indirectly, over time. The phrase he uses to describe this is "slow violence". This concept of "slow violence", which complicates conventional notions of violence as visible acts of confrontation, continues to open new channels of inquiry in postcolonial studies.[55] Nixon's work has made possible, for instance, the framing of environmental pollution by extractive capitalism in the Global South as a form of violence that is possibly more insidious in its impact than conventional violence. "Slow violence" allows us to see the human and nonhuman casualties of environmental pollution as indistinguishable in their mutual experience of degradation by imperialism and capitalist exaction. In this way, one can conceive of the social afflictions wrought by the effects of oil extraction in the Niger Delta, namely ecological devastation, inequitable distribution of wealth from natural resources, and geopolitical marginalisation as forms of violence. These are the concerns that the texts I analyse in this book frame as forms of violence, inflicted by the technologies of oil extraction in the Niger Delta as well as the neoliberal politics that enables them. If these incongruities can be framed as a form of violence – slow violence – it follows therefore that attempts at resisting such conjunctures, imaginatively and politically, might also feature within the purview of violence. Thus, the tropes of violence, both the unseen and the resistant, continue to reverberate throughout the texts that capture the oil encounter. This is what I frame in this book as "Petroculture" in the Niger Delta. Nixon offers insights for thinking through the oil-inflected environmental aesthetics in the literary and filmic depictions of the Niger Delta.

In considering Nixon's ideas to understand the petroculture of the Niger Delta, this book examines the following questions: How do we frame acts of violence as a form of environmentalism? What does it mean to consider violence a contradictory mode of environmentalism, one that is at once radically instructive and insidious, that bespeaks righteous indignation and operates in a climate of exploitative opportunism, both provoked and exacerbated by the damage done to the environment of the Niger Delta? What sets of meaning might this environmentalism of the poor (insurgent violence) elicit when conceived as engendered by oil extraction after many years of negligence and monumental corruption? How might one extricate environmental discourse from its abstractions in scientific discourse and deep ecological musing – otherwise known as "full-stomach environmentalism"[56] – to make it speak anew in a Niger Delta context of petro-induced environmental pollution, geopolitical upheaval and social disintegration?

Byron Caminero-Santangelo's attention to the questions of place in Africa in *Different Shades of Green: African Literature, Environmental Justice and Political Ecology* (2014) is similarly illuminating. For him, postcolonial ecocriticism needs to pay attention to how environmental issues inextricably link other axes of power that interpellate the previously colonised both historically and ontologically. The "unjust forms of imperial development and extraction that...position Africa as a certain kind of place in the world" are, for Caminero-Santangelo, what stimulate African environmental literature. They bring into dialogue the socio-political commitment to place and the ethical imagination of ecology in the struggle for justice, resulting in "an open-ended conception of resistance". [57] The literary works that I discuss in this book are illustrative of this assessment; they instantiate ecological responses of resistance to resource extraction in the indigenous landscapes of the Niger Delta. In staging protests against the ecological and social degradation of local environments, the works stop short of prescribing what form of justice, or what strategy of resistance, is appropriate to the conditions foregrounded. Rather, the texts portray various forms of violence, metaphoric and metonymic, as representative strategies that lay bare the true cost of extraction to the ecological wellbeing of their environments.

Cajetan Iheka's *Naturalizing Africa: Ecological Violence, Agency and Postcolonial Resistance in African Literature* (2018) is another text whose theorising of the "aesthetics of proximity" in African literature considers the intersection of humans with their environments in instances of oppression, resistance and agency.[58] For Iheka, this aesthetics consists of "a spatial sense of nearness" and similarity, by which the African environments are constituted as spaces of shared existence for humans alongside other forms of life, as well as sites of entanglement in which human life is nonhierarchically enmeshed with nonhuman lives in the postcolonial context of ecological justice.[59] Moreover, as Iheka cautions, "postcolonialism needs to be attuned to the ecological implications of colonial and neo-colonial oppression and ensure that its responses are not complicit in the problems it seeks to address".[60] This is because the dimensions of closeness and similarity are ontological and ethical, conferring, among other qualities, "distributed agency" and "indistinction between human and nonhuman entities".[61] One of the effective ways of attuning postcolonialism to the imperatives of ecology is to read for the fluid manner in which the idea of "people" limns beyond its semantic meaning to encompass the nonhuman.[62] Iheka draws on Timothy Morton's call to "treat many more beings as people while deconstructing our ideas of what counts as people".[63] This deconstruction entails an ecological reading of "people" that "intertwines the human with the birds, fish, wild animals, and their surroundings".[64] To be sure, Iheka does not privilege the nonhuman over the human, nor does he relativise the tremendous deprivations that characterise human life in the marginal spaces of the postcolonial world, such as Nigeria's Niger Delta. Rather, he argues that an ecological reading that focuses on human suffering and corollary acts of resistance needs also to take into account the ecological impacts of resistance; the agency of the oppressed must be cognisant of nonhuman interests.[65] In the epilogue, where I analyse Zina Saro-Wiwa's *Karikpo Pipelines* project, I show how Iheka's idea of the cognisance of nonhuman interests bears out. Bringing together human and nonhuman elements in the form of masquerades and bare bodies, Zina's art gestures to environmental interconnection that limns beyond human needs, encompassing the ethos of spirituality and shared value in which nature's agency is privileged outside of human action.

This book involves a close reading of the selected poetry collections, video film and photographs. Although the selected primary texts are multi-generic and mediated through the vehicle of writing, video film and image, the trope of violence with which they engage is what links them together. Nevertheless, it is pertinent to address the exclusion of prose fiction from this book. At least two reasons can be adduced for this omission. The first is the overconcentration of prose fiction in postcolonial ecocriticism.[66] Second, on the Niger Delta more specifically, there has been a significant attention to prose fiction scattered among books and journals, focusing on such novels as Gabriel Okara's *The Voice* (1970); Isidore Okpewho's *Tides* (1993); Tanure Ojaide's *The Activist* (2006);[67] Kaine Agary's *Yellow-Yellow* (2006);[68] and Helon Habila's *Oil on Water* (2010).[69] These scholarly works on fiction offer important insights into how the violence of extraction is made legible. And yet, while attention is rightly drawn to the ways in which prose fiction insists upon the larger ecological needs of the habitat, some of these studies, however, centre the individual protagonist as the agent or catalyst of ecological struggle and justice, even while being "cognisant of nonhuman interests in the struggle for ecological justice".[70] In another instance prose fiction is seen to exhibit "constructive militant discourse" but also through a rather overdetermined character positioning, focalising "ideology and agency".[71] In extending on these important studies, I focus on how poetry, film and photographs afford a particular form suited to thinking about violence and the oil ecology in a way that positions local environment as protagonist; its ally is the community (not individual character) in the struggle for ecological justice.

In the three chapters that follow, I examine poetry as an otherwise private literary form that enters the public arena of social justice advocacy and environmentalism. Poetry is thus shown to engage the political and ethical dimensions of violence that oil extraction inscribes in the locality of the Niger Delta. The film, studied in the fourth chapter, tells the story of youth militancy; although it appears at first to represent a spectacular form of violence, it is concerned with making visible the slow violence that underlies the spectacular. The photographs that I briefly discuss in the epilogue depict the rubble from a violent immediate past and imagine a future beyond the violence of oil extraction and the sensational violence that marks how the Niger Delta is represented in mainstream media discourse, as we encountered in the prologue. Taken together, the book investigates strands of violent ecotrope within the contexts of the oil encounter and the social realities of environmental concerns that generate their narratives. Among other strategies, I examine how the artists, within the different genres, deploy language and visual codes to negotiate tropes of violence and the insurrectionary possibilities that an eco-justice critique might catalyse. I propose that the works assembled here implore the reader to probe further, to rethink the forms of violence and the sphere of subversive articulations that operate, to make visible this violence in the site of oil extraction in the Niger Delta.

Following from the prologue and the introduction, this book includes four main chapters and an epilogue. Chapter 1 examines how two ineluctable phenomena of geography and temporality, both as forms of knowledge and as dimensions of lived experience, converge in the depictions of the Niger Delta. This chapter consists of two main parts. Using the writings of an earlier writer, John Pepper Clark, to stage a literary historiography, the first part examines how the human–nature relationship is conceived in what is framed as a landscape of pre-oil modernity in the Niger Delta. Further, this historiography is deployed to map and track a certain transition to the present writing, noting how the human–nature relationship that shapes the conceptions of nature in earlier writings is destabilised by the oil incursion. The chapter then discusses two contemporary poetry writings, Ebi Yeibo's *A Song for Tomorrow and Other Poems* (2003) and Nnimmo Bassey's *We Thought It Was Oil But It Was Blood* (2002), as main texts to explicate the ways that this oil incursion attenuates the human–nature relationship.

While Chapter 1 reflects on the notion of place, a rural lifeworld in which the human–nature relationship is altered by the extraction of a natural element, oil, Chapter 2 examines the figurations of fire in Ifowodo's *The Oil Lamp*, depicting how ecological injustice bears out in the Niger Delta. Two figurations of fire emerge in the poetry collection. Firstly, fire is material and vagrant, destroying everything in its path. Secondly, fire tropes beyond the physical to foreground the ugliness of power and the hollowness of democracy that is corrupted by oil wealth. Together, the poems present fire as lodged in geopolitical contestations. In Western epistemology, the Promethean allegory embeds emancipation and justice. However, this ideal is not universal; its intrinsic logic becomes inverted in postcolonial Nigeria. The otherwise emancipatory force signifies as an accomplice of neoliberal circuits of destructive extraction.

Chapter 3 extends the discussion to examine the relationship between the Niger Delta and the nation state in which it is situated. This chapter investigates the work of two poets, Tanure Ojaide and Ibiwari Ikiriko, as an appraisal of a fraught nationalism in Nigeria, a nationalism conceived and mobilised around the revenue that accrues from oil extraction in the Niger Delta. Ojaide and Ikiriko, I argue, question the politics of this petronationalism through subversive acts of historiography, ones that narrate an insurrectional poetic of subnational ethic, within which the existence of oil is inscribed. The poets engage recent historical events of the oil encounter in Nigeria – events that emerge as tremendous catastrophes with political and environmental consequences. I explore the representational strategies that each of the poets employs to imagine the oil's presence in this landscape, a neoliberal atmosphere where oil's commodification intimately intertwines and destabilises the ethical life of communities living in proximity to the oil installations. In their attempts to create an alternative history from the incongruous reality that confronts their creative vision, each of the poets deploys a literary motif of the biographical to explore these issues, presenting this environment and its myriad problems as an extended narrative of the self.

Using a Nollywood (Nigerian) film *The Liquid Black Gold* (2010) as its analytical text, Chapter 4 identifies and discusses an intricate climate of geopolitical dissension that attends the forms of environmentalism that oil extraction elicits. The chapter discusses two forms of violence: violence as a form of civil disobedience and violence as a parallel commodity, the latter being analogous to the oil commodity. Violence features as a currency, circulating both as exchange for the oil resource, and as a guaranteed access to the wealth that oil brings. Indeed, the atmosphere of agitation and rebellious mass action that the conjunctures of oil extraction engender ensure that only those who can afford this commodity of violence, either as militant resistance groups, state repressive forces, or those who flout environmental standards to maximise profit, have access to the increasingly militarised oil resource in the region.

The concluding epilogue takes as its point of departure prevailing iterations of the Anthropocene to discuss the ways in which recent post-oil envisioning in the Niger Delta might enable us to approach the Anthropocene as a profound actuality of place. The photographs reflected upon in this concluding chapter evince how the earth, nature and all possibilities of life crumble under the sign of oil, bearing witness to the series of events that mark the culmination of the world's end. Yet at the same time, as I argue, thinking new regimes of energy requires a deliberate attempt to begin from the rubble of the incumbent regime of oil and to envision a world beyond oil, reading apocalyptic realism as an organising trope by which anthropogenic climate change is apprehended. The site of oil extraction is shown to be a rebuttal to the abstracting tendencies of the Anthropocene discussion, intertwined with textures of the real, and evincing devastations of apocalyptic proportions that render all scientific projections anachronistic. The apocalyptic future projected as a possible or imminent occurrence is already a quotidian reality in the oilscape of the Niger Delta. It is these textures of the real and the concrete that constitute what I call apocalyptic realism in the work of Zina Saro-Wiwa.

1 The Niger Delta: Temporality, extraction and the literature of environmental justice

> Poetry and visuals lend their voice to civil protests and other forms of civil disobedience which are launched to sensitise and elicit international sympathy and support for the demand for a clean and healthy environment for the citizens of the Niger Delta.[72]

In the introduction, I attempted to theorise the literary imagination of the Niger Delta as an articulation of a place-based, place-specific form of petroculture. The oil encounter in the Niger Delta is not the official encounter at the point of extraction but, rather, the unofficial encounter, with the side effect of extraction. That is, it is not about oil companies and those who work for them, but about a very different kind of encounter at the sites of oil spills and gas flares, the presence of pipelines and signboards, and how all of these intrude on everyday life and interrupt notions of freedom and justice for local communities and their environment. The dual cultural spheres in which literary creativity operates in the Niger Delta straddle environmental consciousness and petro-imaginings, presenting the art form as a literature of petro-environmentalism. In this chapter, I unpack some of these assumptions by proposing two interlinked phenomena of geography and history – both of which constitute forms of knowledge and dimensions of experience of place – that structure the representation of the Niger Delta.

The chapter consists of two parts. Using the works of JP Clark, a pioneering writer from the Niger Delta region, the first part of the chapter stages a literary historiography of environmental/landscape representation in the literature of the Niger Delta. I examine how the human–nature relationship is conceived in what emerges as pre-oil modernity in the Niger Delta.

In the second part of the chapter, I draw on this historiography to map and track the transition to the present, through reading Ebi Yeibo's *A Song for Tomorrow and Other Poems* (2007) and Nnimmo Bassey's *Thought It Was Oil But It Was Blood* (2002). I note how the human–nature relationship in earlier writing is thus destabilised by the oil incursion. My intention is to show how the local landscape, while offering a spatial context and cultural milieu to the writer's creative imagination, indexes the precariousness of everyday life, even in the years that precede the incursion of petroleum extraction in the 1960s. What the literature provides, therefore, is a cultural landscape that resonates with what David Goldberg describes as "the generalisability of precarity, the proliferation of the conditions of precarious possibility".[73]

The Niger Delta is a terrain of mangrove forests and swamps with networks of estuaries, labyrinthine creeks and tributaries that crisscross the wetlands where the Niger River empties into the Atlantic Ocean. Historically, this environment has always nourished the creativity of writers – poets, novelists, dramatists and memoirists – from this bioregion. Such place-based vision is, of course, not peculiar to the Niger Delta. However, this particular landscape inspires a peculiar aesthetic that is marked by existential yearnings, engendered in the earlier writings by what figures as a hostile geography. The landscape of the Niger Delta in all its luxuriance, beneficence and magisterial force gives colour to the aesthetic choices that constitute the literature of this locale. Writers such as John Pepper Clark and Gabriel Okara found inspiration from the Niger Delta, deploying images fashioned out of the material textures of lived experience.

In the 1960s writings of JP Clark there emerges a conception of the natural world that surrounds human existence as a living object beyond human comprehension, mystical in its interpellation of the human subjects, exerting an agential force so powerful it is shown to strip human subjectivity of atomistic will. In making this claim, I consider how this particular way of conceiving nature counterintuitively sets the stage for the redemptive logic of development petromodernity promises – precisely because it holds the potential of freeing the human subject from the vagaries of an intractable nature and the precariousness of provincial existence.

Take the poem "Streamside Exchange" (1964) in which Clark dramatises a conversation between a child and a weaverbird, with nature as the register of the exchange:

> Child: River bird, river bird
> Sitting all day long
> On the hook over grass
> River bird, river bird,
> Sing to me a song
> Of all that pass
> And say,
> Will mother come back today?
> Bird: You cannot know
> And should not bother;
> Tide and market come and go
> And so shall your mother.[74]

Through the synthesis of nature and culture in the images of "tide" and "market", the poem reflects on the transience of life and its subjection to the corrupting power of time. Here the human subjects, child and mother, are stripped of agency and brought under the vagaries of nature's power and mystery, for the child "cannot know/ And should not bother" about the return of its mother. Nor is the mother's demise comprehensible to the child, given the mysterious ways in which the world works. Even the knowledge of this life's mystery, that is, the truth of its drudgery, eludes the human child. Hence, another one of nature's agents instructs the child on this knowledge: the bird. Through the child's eye of the persona, the reader encounters the "neglected and incomprehensible details of everyday life".[75] This narrative of ordinary provincial life tropes on nature as a mystifying force that dictates the fate of the human subject suggests, counterintuitively, the need for a reappraisal of humanity's relationship to this landscape under a different condition of being.

In Clark's play, *The Raft,* also published in 1964, four lumbermen – Ibobo, Olotu, Kengide and Ogro – are set adrift on an ill-fated boat down one of the creeks of the Niger Delta, leading to their certain doom:

> IBOBO: I don't call that anything, Ogro simply croaks
>   Croaks; that's all
> OLOTU: He can croak
>   For all I care, and as for Kengide
>   He just sits there like some foul-smelling
>   He-goat at the fireside mauling away
>   At the world between his teeth, while you Ibobo
>   Babble about who's a canary and who's not.
>   But in the meantime, what happens to the raft? Or
>   Is it because none of you has a single log
>   In it that your heart cuts very little?
> OGRO: And we are water-logged here
>   In Osikorobo – the confluence of all
>   The creeks!
> OLOTU: The drain pit of all the earth,
>   Or are you too caught by fear to say it?
> KENGIDE: With the swift ebb tide coming
>   And some better lot, we ought to get out
>   Before the sun goes down.[76]

Unable to steer their log-bearing vessel to its destination, all four men are portrayed as bad-tempered and querulous, and this distracts them from their more formidable adversary, the incomprehensible wet labyrinthine landscape along which they drift: the result is their ultimate drowning. The dystopian play depicts a tragic reality that attends everyday human existence in the Delta environment. The superstitious traditional beliefs of the four men, the swampy terrain of the waters upon which they drift, the darkness and their ill-tempered manners converge to destroy all four of them. In the above extracts, the writer's creative preoccupation is with existential and metaphysical angsts borne out of a precarious human existence in relation to the superior force of nature. Nature and environment thus embody a special regime of power in relation to which the human is completely subservient. For the human, therefore, existence in this landscape is bare, akin to Giogio Agambem's notion of the "bare life",[77] but in this present context marked by quotidian drudgery, bordered on all sides by a hostile terrain from which relief is impossible, except through wishful escapism or self-extermination ideations. To be sure, the human– nature relationship that one gleans from the quoted texts is merely secondary, a consequence of the focus on the human condition. This is consistent with the modernist preoccupation in early modern African writing of the twentieth century, which is modelled on the teachings of European educators. Moreover, the focus on existentialism borne out of the immediate geography produced ideas about nature that counterintuitively inspired longings for nature to be urgently subdued, to allow human development to take root. One gets the impression that oil exploration, at the time it began, was a timely intervention, because the relationship that existed between the human subject and the non human natural world was no longer mutually beneficial; the relationship was profoundly hierarchical, with humanity at its lower end. Invariably the thesis of humanity living in subsistent sufficiency within nature's beneficence was an increasingly untenable one; the human–nature relationship needed reconfiguration, a rethinking in the face of changing realities. Little wonder then that oil extraction clothed in industrial modernity – and all its dubious promises of human and environmental development – came as a matter of utmost relief to contain nature's unwholesome influence and recalibrate that uneven relationship for the benefit and in the name of material progress. How then did this arrangement become counterproductive, resulting in a vision of hopelessness, even if attuned to environmental justice?

Time, chronotope and the problem of historicity in Ebi Yeibo's A Song for Tomorrow

Ebi Yeibo's poetry collection, *A Song for Tomorrow* instantiates how oil incursion into the Niger Delta attenuates the human–nature relationship. Beginning with the title of his collection, Yeibo invests time with agency, a hopeful quality that hints at certain redemptive potential. For instance, using the phrase "since then",[78] the poet implicates time as an agential entity with which petro-incursion has brought about change, a dystopia that attends the consequences of oil extraction in the Niger Delta. However, what one gleans from the text is a fissure of historicity in that what confronts the poet's fictive possibility is a reality (of oil extraction) so overwhelming it confounds Yeibo's creativity, resulting in fragmentation, narrative incoherence, and contradictions in point of view.

There is a sense of time-bound hopefulness invested in the phrase, "a song for tomorrow". In the collection is the sense that life, hope and expectations are organised and negotiated around the notion of futuristic time, but one that is imminent, on the cusp. Two specific sections, namely "night" and "twilight",[79] reinforce this sense of imminence, of temporality about to unleash its agency. Night and twilight also connote a sense of ending, retreat and relaxation or recharge: night is a time to retire from the day's activity, and twilight suggests sundown heralding nightfall or, in other words, endings to recuperate. This recuperation involves recollection through memory or an awareness of history in a bid to take stock, to account for, and understand the scheme of things. Taken together, the two parts strike the reader as an envisioning, a recollection or reimagining of the past, unfolding a way of reassessing the situation, a way of scripting the historicity of the social and environmental crisis wrought by oil extraction, with a view to making amends or prognosticating possibilities for the future.

In discussing how historicity adumbrates in Yeibo's poetry, Mikhail Bakhtin's theory of the chronotope provides a useful method of reading. Bakhtin defines the chronotope as the intrinsic connectedness of temporal and spatial relationships artistically expressed in literature. Although this relationship is fictive in an imaginative work of art, it mobilises the concrete textures of the real and the dimensions of the everyday inhabited by the writer. Thus, Yeibo's deployment of the metaphor of time engages the lived senses of history's past, present and future that leave their imprints of memory and experience.

For Bakhtin, the chronotope provides a way of seeing the connections between the past and present, to understand the necessity of "place in this past in the unbroken line of historical development".[80] It is a past reimagined and invoked to make sense of the present. Bakhtin also talks about the importance of the concrete conceptions of place and locality in historicity, noting how the imagination is populated with concrete textures of locality and everyday existence. This, he describes as "chronotopic visualising of locality and landscape, [which] saturates landscape with time – creative, historically productive time".[81] Time as vestige of history is also part of Bakhtin's interest in the discourse of the chronotope. Bakhtin writes that historical time – past, present and future – must have concrete necessity and human relevance in the creative imagination, lending itself to a concrete vision for the betterment of the human condition. The recuperation of the past must be creatively effective in "determining the present", producing a "particular direction for the future, and, to a certain degree, predetermines the future". In effect, the past must be creatively "revealed as necessary and productive under the conditions of a given locality", thereby humanising this locality and transmuting "a portion of terrestrial space into a place of historical life for people".[82]

The Niger Delta is the chronotope of Yeibo's figurations of time. Its time and space form the subject of his narration, in which a tripartite relation of local human subjectivity, environment and the history of oil extraction converge. In deploying the metaphor of time, the locality of the Niger Delta landscape is by no means divorced from the subject of petromodernity. It is this physical locality of the Delta, imaginatively conceived, that gives visible expression to time's cadences in Yeibo's work. In the poem "Testament", time is virtual and imaginative, but it is also conceived materially:

> The rainbow in the sky
> Overwhelms the eye
> And humanity crumbles
> On a platter of nothing
> Since then no candles
> Have ever lit our paths:

We grope and gape ahead
With treble timidity; summoning
Conscious grit, like fishermen
Paddling through water hyacinth
Or a drained old man
Contending with gruelling gristle.[83]

In the first stanza there seems to be an intentional transposition of meaning, a conscious alteration of the allegorical signification of "the rainbow" – assumed a metaphor of hope and of rebirth – to create a vision of temporality through which the persona witnesses to a dystopian experience wrought by time. Through the manipulation of this imagery, the poet brings to the poem an imagined past juxtaposed with an inexplicable present. Although this dystopian vision is evident in the *now*, in the angst-ridden present, it nevertheless derives from some imagined past. Here the poet seems to gesture to a particular new historicist hermeneutic of judging the past in the light of the present. With the recurring phrase of "since then", the poet implicates this imagined past as the traceable source of human suffering in the present:

Since then our senses
Have ever played the plague:
Either incoherent or numb or both
Like skeletons, nibbled neat and dry,
Pleading, unsure, betrayed, thrashed bare.[84]

Moreover, it is not time alone that unleashes its effect, its superior and brutal force upon humanity; time also mobilises other human and non human forces, hence:

…the gods too
Paddle in the same canoe
Having shut their windows:
And the once potent libations
We once poured with tingling testament
Now pay less than gutter-water
In this ghoulish valley
Like mere ashes
When fire closes her eyes.[85]

The gods and the ancestors who once traversed the landscape have abandoned their progenies by "shut[ting] their windows" and the heaving harvest, which the people's libation to the magisterial forebears once assured, has since lost its purchase. But the poem is not only about lamentation; it also frames a narrative that projects hope, one celebrated in the possibilities that the future holds, a future imagined here as tomorrow:

So we learn a new song
Like children learning to walk –

With unsteady, uncertain steps –
For a new tomorrow.[86]

At the same time, the poet invokes powerful imagery of "the rainbow" to instantiate a redemptive development vision for the locality. The metaphor of rainbow also serves to reinforce tropes of time past and time connecting to the subject of hope. This symbolism runs through the entire poem. The image of rainbow as signifier of hope represents an analogy with the biblical rainbow in the Genesis story of Noah, signifying hope and regeneration for humankind.[87] However, in the context of the Niger Delta, the rainbow is the antithesis of hope; for it attends a reality of failed promises and misplaced optimism in the thinking that the discovery of oil would translate into wealth for all. The biblical rainbow does not correspond with the Niger Delta situation: hence, it "overwhelms the eye" and "crumbles" "humanity" "on a platter of nothing".[88]

Nevertheless, the persona seems to suggest that futuristic optimism laced with a song for an imagined future imbues the future with redemptive potential. It depends on the resolution of the crisis of the present, to usher in a better future for the unborn. Writing the foreword for Yeibo's poetry collection, James Tsaaior notes that this song for tomorrow suggests symbolically: "an endless, and, perhaps, ageless song that defines and redefines temporal boundaries and orchestrates the fluidity of history". It "invades the past, dredges and unmasks it as a strategy for distilling invaluable morals that can yield relevance for today and tomorrow".[89] Much as these indicate a certain eschatological vision of endings and possible beginnings in a futuristic Delta, there is a sense of apprehension that pervades the poem. This explains why "Since then.../ We grope and gape ahead/ With treble timidity.../ Pleading, unsure, betrayed, thrashed bare...".[90] Taken together, the lines articulate what Fátima Vieira (echoing Tom Moylan) calls a "critical dystopia".[91] It registers and comments on the social, political and ecological conditions in the locality of oil extraction.

The poem is not all lamentation; it instils a measure of stubborn hope stimulated by "a new tomorrow".[92] Vieira says that critical dystopia is a creative way of foregrounding a negation, while at the same time proffering alternatives that offer hope "for humanity to escape" from a particular socio-historical condition, such as Yeibo's poem distils in this collection. Vieira argues that critical dystopias derive from the same social dreaming that takes impetus from utopian literature, in the sense that literary utopia is a representative strategy for questioning reality and the present.[93]

In the poem "Barren Rivers", Yeibo appears to harken to this utopian imagining of a stable, orderly past as a way of questioning the dissonant present. There is merit to quoting the poem at length:

YESTERDAY
How can we forget
The stirring songs of crickets

That ushered us
To the open hands of dawn?
How can we forget
The warm dews that paved
Untrodden paths to the shore?
The hooks and nets we carried
On padless heads;
The bare feet on which we strutted;
The bilge water we baled?
How can we forget
The fresh breath of fishes
That splashed in the morning sun;
The turtles that brimmed our meals;
The alligators that crammed our canoes,
Exchanging for tapioca and starch
From Urhobo traders, even
Before noon shone on us?
But TODAY:
Fishermen sweat for nothing
They say:
Oil has poisoned the river.[94]

What one gleans from the poem is an imaginative impasse, an incredulity that results in unreliable witnessing. Precisely when the persona attempts to engage with the present setting of the Delta, one permeated by the effects of oil extraction, the poem slips into fragments and conjectures, and this makes his poetic witnessing become unreliable. The facticity presented before the poetic imagination is an incomprehensible one. The poem captures a narrative in which the persona identifies with a pre-oil Niger Delta. Here, the persona speculates about a world of harmony, abundance and peace, one in which oil extraction had not destroyed all that held society in cultural and ecological cohesion. In a sense, Yeibo's imagination in the poem straddles two epochal visions – of an imaginary glorious past and of a mystifying present – to create a narrative that instantiates what Niyi Osundare called a "comparing [of] the glories of yesteryears with the frustrations of today".[95] Both are juxtaposed in conversation to produce an appraisal of the environmental destruction that petro-incursion has wrought on the Niger Delta.

The ideas articulated are contingent upon three lexical items: "we", "us" and "they": these pronouns inflect important meanings in the poem. The words "we" and "us" are at odds with the distancing tone that the third-person plural pronoun "they" conjures up in the last stanza. The poetic voice has tended to identify with a past conceived as "Yesterday" in the way they inscribe themself within the narrative. Here, the mnemonic derives from a sense of habitual experience; hence, the identification with the embodied history reconstructed through "we" and "us" as markers of belonging. However, in the last stanza "But TODAY", the persona appears to dissociate from the reality into which the narrative translates, deploying the third person plural "they" as a gesture of extrication from the incongruous environment that confronts the imaginative possibility. Employing the phrase "they say" makes the narrative voice come across as conjectural and unreliable. Such projection of facelessness and unreliability in narrating the oil encounter resonates with Canadian cultural critic Robert Fulford's pithy metaphor, the "cracked mirror of modernity".[96]

Fulford surmises that in a chaotic atmosphere of incoherencies and mystification to which the modern world gravitates, there emerges "the unreliable narrator, the storyteller for the age of doubt and incredulity. The modern temperament quickens to stories that are splintered in this way: when we read [such] works…we stare into the cracked mirror of modernity."[97] This last phrase captures the way in which Yeibo attempts to grapple with the social reality of the present, resulting in a fragmented poetic vision – a vision that resists historicity. The tone of the narrative persona comes across as one of denial of the present reality, and this compels the flow of the poem in a way that quickens the lines of the last stanza. This quickening of the poetic flow is also evident in the structure of the poem. The fragmented last stanza corroborates the poet's fragmentary vision of the present reality. This fragmentation becomes symptomatic of an unreliable narrator. In his attempt at bearing witness to the present conditions, the persona imagines a particular kind of time: psychological time.

Bakhtin notes that psychological time "possesses subjective palpability and duration, [that engenders the] depiction of danger, [and] agonising suspense".[98] I would add that, unlike Bakhtin, Yeibo is unable to give concrete localisation to time's presence in this poem. This is because the "psychologically coloured" vision that confronts his imagination overwhelms his signification into fragments and narrative incoherence. It is only through the mediation of language, that is, the switch between pronouns of "we" and "they", that the reader is able to establish the meaning of the material condition depicted in the poem. Indeed, these forms of fragmentary vision and narrative incoherence work to undercut the poet's attempt at capturing concrete reality in this collection. This can be read as an indication of the mystifying reality wrought by the oil encounter in the Delta. The late capitalism that heralded oil extraction in the Niger Delta began to inspire narratives that were no longer straightforward and philosophical about life, such as one finds, for instance, in the early works of JP Clark.[99] In contrast, the oil encounter spawns in the writer's imagination narratives that favour self-reflexive ironies, discouragements and scepticism. These works refract a sense of postmodernist disorderliness, chaos and, paradoxically, exciting industrial activities in close proximity to local abjection; all of these refract the real, lived experience of being in the oil sites of the Delta.

Take for instance the poem "Dry Season", where the poet juxtaposes images of barrenness with those of prodigious harvest at the instance of the wealth that oil generates from the region:

> It is no time for celebration, friends
> When barrenness gnaws at naked souls
> Like desperate wild rats in a wizard's tale
> And a nation crawls on an aching belly
> To the wilderness of nowhere…
> And I suppose still
> The drought and harmattan
> Are sure spellbound
> When false rains throw a hearty party
> Of live charcoals and flaming brimstones
> For laughing seedlings
> And unknown tendrils and their dreams.[100]

Although the poem draws significant numbers of images from nature, one notices that things no longer converge at the centre, where nature exercises agency and power over human subjectivity. The atmosphere of incongruous human, material and environmental suffering that the poem narrates is amenable to a resigned doubt directed at some imagined treacherous entity, one that holds access to the commonwealth for its personal aggrandisement. Scepticism is a powerful tenor with which the poem opens: "It is no time for celebration, friends". This infuses the theme of resistance with a measure of vibrancy and determination to achieve change in an atmosphere of economic exploitation. In fact, scepticism appears to be a way of staging protests against forms of social disaffection. The persona seems to suggest that imprudence, which he frames to be the absence of scepticism at this historical moment, is dangerous for the local human community, precisely because it has, so far, led to a blind alley, to "nowhere", and produced only nothingness, "drought" and "barrenness". Thus, the poet suggests that this anti-utopia, laced in a song for tomorrow, will prompt humanity to begin asking searching questions that will lead to betterment.

Yeibo draws on the metaphor of barrenness, where he mobilises a seasonal time in tropical Africa: the "dry season" and the "harmattan" that it heralds to describe an atmosphere of dashed hope and failed promises:

> So when heavy clouds gather again
> In the deep blue sky
> The innocent sky that sings
> Spirited songs of solace across the land
> Do we not cover our ears?
> Do we not choose to be blind?
> Do we not hang belief on a rafter?[101]

Cast in scepticism, this conviction is invested with sarcasm and jest rendered to produce renewed hope and optimism in the poem "Tears in the Home":

> Dictatorship is a hungry guest
> That swallows its host
> Spreading darkest shadows
> Where no sun shines…
> May this budding shine
> That now twinkles in the timid tenor
> Right inside the black tunnel
> Console the crying creeks
> Then clear the harrowing haze
> That hangs in the hinterland.[102]

What we have is an intimation of firm resilience articulated in the register of futuristic hope. Yeibo's optimism is not baseless, even if deriving from a fragmented, mystifying present. Rather it has tended to be rooted in a utopian vision of the future built on the possibilities that he sees in the present: the courage of the local communities in standing up to the otherwise overwhelming power of Big Oil and government.

His vision of the future refuses to be distorted in the hopelessness caused by corrupt leadership: a cabal of "these patriots", who have "played on us" a "horrendous hoax" and left in their wake "O-F-F-E-N-S-I-V-E" remains "like [the biblical] Cain's offering".[103] Nevertheless, Yeibo's attempt to construct an alternative path to redemption for his people is modest and incremental:

> May this stirring sun
> That now strips naked
> Scrap-iron scoundrels swindling
> With starched khaki
> Mop up the maddening murk
> And stem the stream of tears
> O let the chorus of light shower
> Let the showers of laughter
> Burst open bowels of disinherited barns
> That still litter the land
> Let the chorus of saints
> Bury the canister of lies,
> Daggers of memory, with ancient harvests
> Let cringing cocks crow again.[104]

Yeibo remains true to specific creative boundaries of realist literature, which enables him to work with facts, material history and social reality, all of which he de-familiarises and turns into resistance, a way of producing alternative possibilities to move society forward. The poet makes a compelling temporal connection between the past and the present as a way of prognosticating the future. His imagination and projections of the future, while not unfounded, seem quite conjectural as they are premised on hope, that is, the budding horizon of the *real* available to the poet's fictive possibilities.

In the poem "Twilight", this material sense of imagining the future further demonstrates a modest optimism and hope of rebirth:

> Tomorrow, fresh and fecund.
> Smiles from the world yonder
> Surveys the expansive earth
> With misted eyes
> For a place to perch.[105]

Again, the reader can observe the poet's investment in the possibilities that the future might bring about, even when that sense of hope bears little or no relation to the present situation. Nothing in the present suggests any logical progression to the possibility of an imminent goodness, yet it "smiles from…yonder", although not without "misted eyes". Here is a gesture once again to critical dystopia, infused with a strong utopian impulse that puts despair at bay, even when the latter hovers on the horizon like a brown fog on a wet sunless day.

In the poem, "For My Son Yet Unborn", Yeibo extends this investment in the future, as a product of the emptying of the will in the present. Here the future takes a more material form, invested in the unborn, rather than in the intangible "tomorrow":

> From crimson creeks, I weave
> This song, for like floods
> In a season of showers
> Villains have taken over our shores
> And their acid breath chokes the land
> With mantra of fading dreams…
> That our children may find
> The tickling harmonies of old
> When they come.[106]

In this poem, there is a deliberate ethically positioned articulation of environmentalism, but it will come about only at some point in the future. The observing voice seems completely empty of any agential capability or will, except hopefulness in the future. What we have here is an ultimate dystopia: with "crimson creeks", seashores taken over by "villains", the land completely polluted. By outsourcing the capacity to prevail over these negations, the future in the form of the unborn must look to the past for inspiration and solution. Concerned with giving an account of the present reality to the unborn, the poet connects a genealogical question of patrimony to the ethical responsibility of protecting the local environment. The poet's apprehensions are amplified by doubts concerning the present and faith in a future whose foundation seems to exist only in the realm of wishful conjectures. Here is poesy making a rigorous attempt at constructing the phenomenon of oil extraction on the socio-cultural history of the Niger Delta.

Yeibo's consciousness of time indicates an aesthetic of moving forwards and yet thinking backwards, thereby causing a disruption in the representation of a problematic present. Through the techniques of memorialising, he places his disaffection on the material context of a lived past whose ghosts continue to manifest in the social realities of the present, while providing a template for projecting the future. Yeibo's engagement with these categories of time proceeds from a consciousness of history, even if imaginary. Indeed, as Ime Ikiddeh notes, "every writer...is a historian of his time, the unconscious recorder of the events and the mood of his society. His view of the world...represents at one level a confrontation with the reality of history, past or present";[107] thus, Yeibo's sense of history is a way of witnessing to the social realities occasioned by the timed experience of the oil encounter and its attendant adverse effects on social and ethical life in the locality. To the poet, time is history's force and talebearer. Employing the poetics of time, the landscape of the Niger Delta signifies as trapped in an impasse that is impervious to the present; whose solution might possibly come in the near future, but not without the rallying input from the past. So, in other words, in Yeibo's vision of time, using the Niger Delta as chronotope, the present is profoundly perfunctory; or at best catalytic to the agential will with which he imbues the future, whose potentiality resides in its alliance with the past, conjured up by subjective experience and memory.

In what he calls the "Parables of Time", Ato Quayson reflects on certain protocols of depicting time in literature, highlighting two key dimensions. The first he calls subjective experience, "interpreted and felt by the individuals", and the other is a form of portrayal marked by received "cultural rituals of temporal imagining".[108] These categories resonate with the figurations of time at play in Yeibo's poetry. His metaphor of time is at once subjectively personal and culturally communal. However, this conscious, subjective mode of imagining time can eschew realism, precisely because that does not serve the purpose of the narrative vison, as we have seen in Yeibo's text. Moreover, this explains why, confronted with the real, the poems retreat to some imagined past or a fantasised future, the result of which are fragmentations and an incoherent historicity. In other words, by muting the present and projecting hope unto the future, the poet is able to bend his sense of the past to the will of the future being scripted into being throughout the collection, thereby projecting a logical progression from the present to that future possibility.

This disjuncture is not peculiar to this author. It seems that sites of extraction of natural resources present startling evidence of the wide divide between humanity's march towards progress and hope, and the landscapes of abandonment that follow in the wake of that onward march. I now turn to Nnimmo Bassey, a poet whose work privileges a sense of place as a way of vivifying modernity's disjuncture. His poem offers a way of scripting the historicity of the oil encounter, while at the same time anticipating a future from the environmental rubble of the present. In his collection, *We Thought It Was Oil But It Was Blood*, Bassey creates a narrative out of the urgent condition of the Delta, in which he advocates for effective action against the obnoxious practices of the oil industrial complex, and suggests ways of achieving justice for the environment through collective action from among the people.

Nnimmo Bassey – Thinking from the apocalyptic rubble of the petroleumscape: Towards a transnational petro-environmentalism

The Niger Delta presents for the public mind the extremely negative impact of extractive capitalism on the environment. This bioregion indexes the quintessential site of the apocalyptic future promised by climate change. However, this devastation is already an everyday reality for the local inhabitants. My interest in apocalyptic depictions of the earth's ecology is premised on the ways in which literary imagining in the Niger Delta frames climate crisis as apocalyptic events happening in real time, rather than abstract processes. In other words, literary apocalypticism puts environmental issues in actual contexts rather than in discursive abstractions. I will show how literature, precisely poetry, mobilises metaphors to put abstract processes of the earth's climate changes in graphic contexts as events experienced in the everyday lives of people directly affected by these changes, especially in the Global South.

It is this apocalyptic realism that frames and inspires Nnimmo Bassey's poetry collection, *We Thought It Was Oil But It Was Blood*. Bassey's poetry symbolises what I call "strategic apocalypse" as a means of challenging the continued extraction of fossil fuel that render the planet uninhabitable for human and nonhuman life forms. When we deliberate on the anthropogenic effect on the earth's climate, Bassey invites the reader to think about the local origins of fossil fuels, and about the brutal effects of crude extraction and pollution on everyday life in local environments, as the starting point. In this collection, Bassey inflects climate crisis as a global scourge aided by the tenets of neoliberalism, tenets that abet globalised practices of unchecked and unsustainable exploitation of natural resources in local, indigenous landscapes, such as the Niger Delta. Bassey's poetry suggests that this extractive onslaught needs to be addressed in a unified struggle of collective resistance and subversion, through a well-orchestrated campaign to discontinue what the poet in another context calls "destructive extraction".[109]

In an interview with Amy Goodman and Juan Gonzalez, Bassey states that "the United Nations must begin to pay more attention to what the people of the world are saying, what the people who are impacted by the multiple [climate] crises are experiencing, rather than listening so much to what corporations are saying".[110] He believes that a real solution must be sought; that such a solution is to be "found in the people's summit, the people's space, where people are not beating around the bush. [They are insisting] that we have to stop corporate capture; we have to stop false solutions in terms of selling off forests and cutting off communities from the resources that they need to live". I show how this point forms an important position in the ongoing debates on climate crises. Further, I discuss how Bassey's poetry draws from this pro-people ethic of ecological consciousness to inaugurate a transnational imagining of petro-environmentalism as a way of protesting (and possibly halting) the accelerated human-induced changes to the earth's climate, considered to be driven primarily by extractive capitalism.

Although his campaigns have brought him public recognition and respect, Bassey has also become a bit of an irksome personage to the oil industrial complex. His consistent message to the oil conglomerates is "leave the oil in the ground",[111] since the cost of petroleum around the world has continued to be subsidised by the poor who inhabit the pollution caused by fossil fuel extraction. In his book *Politics of Climate Justice,* South African environmental activist Patrick Bond writes that "Nnimmo Bassey jumped the scale [of climate justice politics] to demand that oil be left in the soil and under the Gulf of Guinea".[112] This demand that oil be left underground in the interest of the environment and peoples around its habitat is what has been termed "Yasunisation".

"Yasunisation" names and describes relatively recent initiatives, through campaigns and activism, to compel and encourage the idea of leaving fossil fuel in the ground, to forestall and "to combat climate change, to preserve biodiversity and to safeguard the livelihoods of the indigenous populations in Ecuador's Amazon region".[113] It is a neologism formed from the name of a national park, Yasuni, in Ecuador. In June 2007, the then Ecuadorian government of President Rafael Correa agreed to leave 850 million barrels of oil (representing 20 per cent of Ecuador's oil reserve) in the Ishpingo-Tambococha-Tiputini (ITT) section of the Yasuni National Park in Amazonian Ecuador. The national park, a rain forest known for its carbon sequestration potentials, lies within the ancestral territory of the Waorani indigenous peoples. Although President Correa's acceptance came with a stipulation (that the international community must compensate Ecuador for its sacrifice of leaving 20 per cent of its oil reserve untapped), the strong implication of this initiative is that it signals the potential creation of a post-oil society in that it provides a sustainable living condition for all, including indigenous peoples.[114] The move to leave oil underground in the interest of indigenous inhabitants and for the protection of biodiversity has become something of an attempt to fashion a climate change policy based on Southern norms and practical realities. Thus, Yasunisation is a transnational campaign to keep oil underground, not only in Yasuni-ITT but also in other places where oil is extracted, places inhabited by mostly poor indigenous peoples and populated by rich biodiversity.

Nnimmo Bassey turns to this Yasunisation initiative for inspiration in his poetry. He draws on such campaigns as a way of instigating an environmental poetics of strategic apocalypse. Bassey believes that through social movements the machinery of environmental pollution can be halted – and possibly reversed. He argues that the poor people living in the oil fields close to where crude oil is extracted should come together and forced the discontinuation of oil production. Then the world would be obliged to go the renewable energy way, for that is the way of the future.

When asked about his decision to take to writing poetry in his environmental activism, Bassey responds:

> I found that in the struggle it's essential to take some aspects of performance. In the African context, a lot of social struggles are carried on the vehicle of poetry and song. And so I began writing poetry seriously in the early 1990s...I found poetry to be very useful in terms of mobilizing resistance, getting people to feel a part of the movement and so some of my poems are not just for people to read quietly, but for people to be part of the reading so that there are calls and responses; so, for example, when I say 'we thought it was oil' the audience responds 'but it was blood'.[115]

In *We Thought It Was Oil But It Was Blood,* Bassey brings into the public sphere issues of social and environmental justice, thus walking a line between commitment to poetry and commitment to environmental activism (performed in poetry). The poetry collection is marked by a tone of defiance and a mood of anger, provoked by the collective deprivation of local people from access to the wealth that extraction of natural resources brings, and the effect on the environment too, which suffers pollution owing to the mindless drilling of pipes into what the poet calls "Mother Earth". Bassey uses the medium of poetry to create a text that presents an environmental rights manifesto. His call for environmental justice at this conjuncture of ongoing conversations on climate change indicts the oil extraction industry. The anthology, which Vanessa Baird describes as "dedicated to campaigning for environmental justice",[116] is a creative effort to capitalise on Bassey's already established stature as an environmental rights activist. Through his poetry, Bassey draws attention to corporate lawlessness and environmental crimes inflicted on local landscapes that bear fossil fuel for the oil industry. He has travelled throughout these parts to see first-hand how the oil extraction industry and other big businesses have destroyed local landscapes, and his account is vivid and actual, even if represented through the fictive and yet compellingly evocative medium of poetry.

Apocalyptic metaphor as critique of petromodernity

In *We Thought It Was Oil* Bassey confronts the reality of fossil fuel extraction with a vision that is discerning and perceptive. His poetry brings into sharp focus "the value of imaginative writing as a site of discursive resistance",[117] useful for questioning the environmentally exploitative attitudes of corporate institutions such as Shell in Nigeria and elsewhere. In *Postcolonial Ecocriticism: Literature, Animals, Environment* (2010), ecocritics Graham Huggan and Helen Tiffin echo fellow Australian Val Plumwood,[118] in insisting that we question the very forms of instrumental reasoning that view nature and non human others as being external [and subject] to human needs, and thus effectively disposable; alternatively, as being in permanent service to humanity, and thus endlessly replenishable.[119] Although their intervention is well informed and critical to rethinking ways of arresting the climate crises that confront the planet, it ought to come with certain contextual extenuations, especially in the case of the rural Global South, places like the Niger Delta and South America's Orinoco Delta depicted in Bassey's poetry collection.

I argue that Bassey stretches this philosophical basis of ecological thinking to useful limits of representational possibilities. While his primary interest is in what he calls "Mother Earth" – the environment – he does not repudiate the utilitarian relevance of nature to local, indigenous people, who must live off the environment. In reading this poetry collection, I substantiate this point in a way that exemplifies how Bassey's activism broadens the somewhat limited models of mainstream ecocriticism, while also fostering a transnational alliance of environmental imagining in the Global South. Bassey's poetry articulates an ecological vision consistent with a concrete praxis pertaining to the environment's cultural relevance to the people who depend on nature for subsistence.

He uses apocalyptic metaphor – a strategic apocalypse – to draw attention to the damages caused by unsustainable oil extraction in the Global South.

Two figurations of apocalypse emerge in the poetry. The first is the poet's figuration of oil as blood to suggest that the continued extraction of fossil fuel inflicts violence and destruction on the environment and local inhabitants of the extraction sites. In the eponymous poem "We Thought It Was Oil", the poet bears witness to a history of indigenous peoples and nature, the earth, entangled in a unified experience of petrocapitalism, as the refrain in the poem suggests:

> We thought it was oil
> But it was blood
> Dried tear bags
> Polluted streams
> Things are real
> When found in dreams
> We see their Shells
> Behind military shields
> Evil, horrible, gallows called oilrigs
> Drilling our souls
> We thought it was oil
> But it was blood...[120]

In this poem modelled on a call-and-response motif of folksong, the poet associates oil with the image of blood to evoke an instance of ecological destruction in the wake of oil extraction. He deploys images of blight, war and death in the form of "blood", "gallows", "black holes", "slaughtered on the slab" and "bright red pool", to give graphic expression to a dystopian vision of the oil encounter. The poet persona puns on the word "Shells" to allegorise the fraught history of environmental protests in Niger Delta, ones that attend the extraction of oil. It is a history that is riddled with violence, destruction and death, culminating in the hanging of the foremost activist Ken Saro-Wiwa. Thus, the poet utilises poetic language to frame this narrative in a way that at once constricts and proliferates meaning. Although the word "Shells" is deployed ambiguously here, meaning is not arbitrarily assigned. It is in the realm of context – historical and political – together with its referent, that the meaning of this signification of "Shell" is realised. The word is associated with military weaponry, denoting the ammunition used in artillery bombardment. Alternatively, shells are the remnants of cartridges to be found in battlegrounds after the exchange of gunfire. But more importantly, "Shells" as it is used in this poem is synonymous with the giant Anglo-Dutch Shell Petroleum Development Company, which operates a large stake of the oil installation in Nigeria. Note that "Shells" is given a capital letter, which suggests that it is a proper noun, but this is also contradicted by the fact that it is in its plural form. The poet indulges with the particular and general and the different uses of the term. Nevertheless, the image of "Shells/ Behind military shields" conjures up an historical moment in Nigeria: the Ogoni tragedy (which the persona hints at in two preceding stanzas) and Shell's involvement (through its liaison with General Sani Abacha's military junta) in the judicial travesty that resulted in the state-orchestrated execution, by hanging, of Ken Saro-Wiwa and the Ogoni Eight. The concrete image of "gallows" in the next line provides added evidence of this historical resonance: as the nine Ogoni activists were hanged in November 1995.

But the poem is not only about recounting the atrocities of oil extraction in the Niger Delta; it is also a narrative of affirmative resistance:

> They may kill all
> But the blood will speak
> They may gain all
> But the soil will RISE
> We may die
> And yet stay alive
> Placed on the slab
> Slaughtered by the day
> We are the living
> Long sacrificed
> We thought it was oil
> But it was blood…[121]

In this stanza, the persona spurs the reader to action and mobilises a personified natural element, the soil, to "RISE" in defiance and confront the petro-induced onslaught on the environment. The apocalyptic impulse of the poem – although situated in the realpolitik of resistance against neoliberal extraction – is imbued with strong religious cadences rooted in the Christian doctrine of resurrection and the afterlife. This perhaps explains the collocation of "soil" and "RISE", suggesting burial and resurrection, and possibly the post-materiality of the ecological consciousness that informs petro-environmentalism. Sule Egya notes that "the accent on RISE dramatizes the hope of an undefeated people", noting that the image of blood refers to "both the oil pumping from the soil and the spilled blood of slain humans", both becoming generative symbols "conflating human and ecological suffering".[122]

I would go so far as to argue that, since humanity and nature are unified in a similar experience of suffering, the poem affirms that collaboration between human and natural entities in fending off the oil-inspired onslaught on their locality will mount a formidable resistance poised to outlast petrocapitalism. In a different context, critic Oyeniyi Okunoye suggests that the poet as activist "consistently identifies with the helpless, the violated and the weak, affirming that they would outlive their oppressors".[123] Using poetry as an alternative vehicle for enunciating instances of the environment in the throes of extractive capitalism, Bassey reverses the trend of written testimony backed by activism. He considers poetry an alternative medium for the articulation of climate justice for poor, indigenous people.

The second strand of literary apocalypse is gleaned from Bassey's poem "When the Earth Bleeds" in which he excoriates the logic of petromodernity:

> I hear that oil
> Makes things move
> In reality check
> Oil makes life stop
> Because
> *The oil only flows*
> *When the earth bleeds*
> A thousand explosions in the belly of the earth
> Bleeding rigs, bursting pipes
> This oil flows
> From the earth's sickbed
> Because
> *The oil only flows*
> *When the earth bleeds*[124]

Employing startling and gripping metaphors such as "bleeding rigs, bursting pipes" and "explosions in the belly of the earth", the author evokes a gut reaction from the reader. Although these images may seem spectacularly dramatic, they operate as apocalyptic realism, for they capture and describe the catastrophic reality of fossil fuel extraction in local environments. Again, the words "apocalypse" and "realism" are so at odds as to seem contrived and contradictory when combined to capture and describe the actual impact of oil-induced pollution in the Niger Delta. Nevertheless, what is presented here is an allegory in which the poet employs concrete metaphors to heighten and estrange the real, to provoke and incite effective action against what emerges as an actual violence, which oil extraction inflicts on the environment. The poem interrogates modernity's promise to put an end to the drudgery of life that is lived outside the sphere of its influence. The poem suggests that this (otherwise) logical dream is an illusion, an empty promise that appears to characterise human existence in places where oil is extracted. Petrocapitalism has negatively affected nature; its logic of accelerated progress through the extraction of oil energy is essentially counterproductive, as it also brings about the accelerated destruction of the very environment that hosts its activities. Indeed, in the end it inflicts violence and death on the earth and its ecosystem.

> The ocean waves bathe our eyes
> But in Ogoniland we can't even breathe
> Because
> *The oil only flows*
> *When the earth bleeds*
> What shall we do?
> What must we do?
> Do we just sit?
> Wail and mope?
> Arise people, Arise
> Let's unite
> With our fists
> Let's bandage the earth
> Because
> *The oil only flows*
> *When the earth bleeds.*[125]

In discussing Bassey's project of environmentalism in this poem, what emerges is a scathing rendition that presents us with a form of lyrical testimony against the hypocrisy of political gatherings under the guise of devising a solution to the climate crisis. In a sense, the poem lends itself to what I consider a persuasive ethical interpretation in the way it tends towards infusing political gatherings, ostensibly in the interest of the earth's climate, with a measure of moral imperative – it suggests that, to halt and possibly reverse accelerated climate change, we must first discontinue the extraction of, and unwholesome dependence on, fossil fuel. Bassey's environmentalism in this poem gives credence to Greg Garrad's claim that "Environmental apocalypticism is not about anticipating the end of the world, but about attempting to avert it by persuasive means".[126]

What fascinates about the poem "When the Earth Bleeds" is the way it breaks with conventions of the written medium. The poem is imbued with a sense of direct speech as if addressing a gathering in a street demonstration. Although the poet persona appears mindful of the poem as primarily a written text, he "consistently employs *speakerly* strategies to point at the oral nature of the signification".[127] This points to the urgency of Bassey's concerns and the earnestness of his attempt to provide the reader with an affective experience similar to that of listening to a live address in a public gathering. Here is a poet with an abiding commitment to the politics of non-silence, putting at the centre-stage of climate deliberations a tangible instance of the planet in peril, by using the sites of oil extraction as examples. As the poem suggests, neither passive lamentation, where we "just sit", "wail" and "mope", nor repeated declamations of environmental devastation are enough to apprehend the destruction that a civilisation based on oil energy continues to inflict on the planet. Further, the poet derides the ostentation of conferences, where delegates are insulated in "halls" and "gardens of stones", and where "ocean waves" add to their insulation from the grim reality of ecological destitution with which some must contend. Therefore, Bassey evokes spectacular images of apocalyptic proportions, as a way of inciting effective action in "bandaging the bleeding earth". Here, then, is a contrast between the pretentions of conference rhetoric and pomp of high-level gatherings, and the actual event of the human-made ecological crisis that is Ogoni in particular, and the Niger Delta in general. Indeed, the poet employs a representational strategy that infuses political debates on climate change with a measure of ethical imperative: Ogoni becomes the open wound that numbs the collective conscience of political discourse on climate justice.

The poet's choice of language, especially in the last stanza, is suggestive of his insurrectionary disposition. The repetition of "Arise" with a capital letter "A" and the lexical item "fists" gesture to the urgency of active and revolutionary involvement. Bassey seems to reinvent an ethos to motivate and empower popular activism – suggesting that street marches and freedom square gatherings are increasingly becoming the legitimate site of critical engagement to achieve justice for the mass of people. Crucially, the poem expresses a certain disenchantment that has less to do with social injustice than with the damage done to the environment, to the earth, by petrocapitalism. And that explains why the poet makes a clarion call to the public not just to reclaim their stolen patrimony, but, first, and most importantly, to "Arise", "unite", and "bandage the earth"; to salve the wounds inflicted by the scourge of oil extraction and hydrocarbon pollution.

Despite the clear moral insight demonstrated by Bassey in identifying the challenges of resource extraction in local landscapes and economies, the writer-activist has tended to be measured in his articulation of resistance and ultimately of justice. For him, the task of rebuilding from the rubble of capitalist exaction from local ecologies lies with the collective, for in the process we not only protect the natural environment but also the economy that it sustains. Take, for instance, his poem titled "Polluted Throats", which signifies two unusual collocates: "pollution", associated with the contamination of a natural environment, and "throat", which is metonymic of human basic need, associated with eating and drinking. The items are in juxtaposition here to point to the twin interest of ecology and economics, which is at the heart of Bassey's environmentalism:

> At the yellow fields
> Of Jacinto
> Zambrano drinks polluted streams
> Sees his rice field die
> Stands back and waits
> He wails: *it may kill us but what can we do?*
> The question that won't run away
> *But what can we do?*
> Something
> That's what we can do
> And must[128]

The poet employs a farmer figure, Zambrano, to stand in for those whose means of existence alongside the local environment is doubly decimated by the effects of resource extraction. The poem expresses how urgent and decisive action can infuse ecological awareness with productive agency and inspire courage, even in a despondent situation where oppressed people throw up their hands in a defeatist relinquishment. Hence, in response to Zambrano's hopeless declaration: *"it may kill us but what can we do?"*, the poet persona inspires hope in the following stanza: "Something/ That's what we can do/ And must." Here the poet is suggesting that even when the odds are overwhelmingly against the oppressed, collective action can be a counterpoint to the powerful ambivalence of capitalism's business-as-usual stance, to challenge the double decimation inflicted on local existence in the throes of resource extraction.

The reticence (or perhaps modesty) intimated in the last stanza is too obvious to ignore. It works powerfully to involve the reader, to implicate the collective and in the process the poem becomes political, for it urges the need to act. Perhaps this sheds light on Jay Parini's claim that "Often enough, poetry gives voice to what is not usually said, and in this sense it becomes 'political'".[129] While the modality of this political action is open to interpretation, the reader can see that passivity and dejection are not a choice, as they come at a double cost to the environment and the local economy. Thus, the open-ended conception of resistance in the poem, as Caminero-Santangelo has noted, indicates that the solution and even the will to act resides squarely with the reader and, therefore, the collective.

In his essay, "Where Is the Now?", historian and postcolonial theorist Dipesh Chakrabarty privileges the pragmatism of an agentive "now" over the ostensible complacency of the political in addressing concerns that confront contemporary modernity. He argues that the manner of "[h]ow we periodize our present is thus connected to the question of how we imagine the political".[130] Chakrabarty insists that

> [E]very imagination of the political entails a certain figure of the now.
> That is why, when we begin by defining the now in a very particular
> way as our first step of analysis, we have in a sense already committed
> ourselves to a certain understanding of the political…For it is only by
> acknowledging the murkiness of the political today that we will configure
> a now so plural as not to be exhausted by any single definition.[131]

I want to use Chakrabarty's pronouncements here to unpack further some possible meaning in this poem, because there is a sense of ambiguity about the metaphor "something", a fascinating referent through which the political affect – interlinking ecology and economics – of postcolonial environmentalism is articulated in the poem. The "thing" evokes a sense of the concrete, but when taken together, "something" suggests vagueness, indeterminacy. However, the tension generated here is a productive one, useful for unpacking the poem further. The "thing" points to the transformative force palpable at the site where the agency of the oppressed meets with the political will of the collective; the vague aspect that "something" elicits points to the open-ended possibilities, a potentially infinite range of action that is possible to take to curb the excesses of extraction capitalism. Bassey uses this term to indicate the primacy of a timely and decisive action geared towards achieving a condition that will bring about the discontinuation of fossil fuel extraction, not only in the interests of nature because of the ecological catastrophe, but also because of its unsustainability for local economies. I argue that indeed the unsaid possibility of "something" in this poem infuses the political with a possibility so powerful as to seem liberating – a gesture to the historical awareness of colonial exploitation and the possibility that this specific instance might just be a vestige of it. Hence, the poem concludes with a more compelling verb "must", to add a note of urgency, to operate as a summons to mobilise and push against the limits of our moral imagination, stimulating the reader into action.

The potential of the collective will to act is further evoked in the poem "Winamorena", where Bassey connects the environmental pollution of an oil-producing town in South America's Orinoco Delta to Nigeria's Niger Delta, in a unified vision of mutual experience. He imagines the landscape of Winamorena as an extension of the Niger Delta:

> Day breaks in a thousand rays
> Tickling my eardrums are tom-toms
> Of distant homes screaming the call
> Of two Deltas pulled apart...
>
> Today let the Deltas unite
> Let kinship defy the seas let
> Love, pains, laughter power the paddles
> As two daybreaks that make a day
> Rolling in my hammock I smell
> Taylor Creek, Stub Creek
> Manamo, Nun, Qua Iboe
> Winamorena beckons Okoroba
> Orinoco calls the Niger
> Swinging from my h'mock
> I see a dance of two deltas.[132]

This is probably the more compelling poem in which Bassey's poetics of transnational petro-environmentalism is realised. His campaign to resist and halt extractive capitalism is not limited to the provincial corners of his local Niger Delta. His vision as performed in this poem transcends geographical borders. It is consistent with what Nixon, in a related context, has described as "site-specific struggles...across national boundaries in an effort to build translocal alliances".[133] The environmentalism of the poor to which Nixon alludes, and which has been prominent in my discussion so far, is in a sense an expression of ethical solidarity for the victims of extractive capitalism, one that leaves in its trail a two-prong form of violence at the sites of resource extraction. I suggest that Bassey's aesthetic of environmental activism is a form of cosmopolitanism that straddles spatial and temporal distances to bring the human condition within one frame of mutual poetic experience.

According to the poem, although the Deltas – the Orinoco in South America and the Niger in southern Nigeria – may be separated geographically from each other, they are intimately connected in a common lived experience of existing side by side with the effects of capitalist extraction; a lived experience in the Global South of the oil encounter that leaves in its wake a polluted environment riven with poverty and a decimated local economy. Bassey sees environmental pollution as a global scourge aided by the obnoxious tenets of neoliberalism, tenets that must be apprehended in a unified struggle of collective defiance and subversion. He seems to be saying that the global exploration – and exploitation – of oil leaves in its wake the same ruinous social and environmental repercussions in local, vernacular landscapes; a disturbing familiarity which makes "Winamorena [in Ecuador] beckon Okoroba [in the Niger Delta, just as] Orinoco [in Venezuela] calls [on] the Niger".[134] Even as the poet persona reclines in a makeshift bed in the creeks of the South American Orinoco Delta, he "smell[s]" the familiar filth of the Nun and Qua Iboe creeks of the Niger Delta. Thus, he calls for "a dance of [the] two Deltas"[135] to mobilise and oppose this exploitative trend of externally inflicted abjection. He believes that globally, people's movements are connected in a unified struggle of the human spirit. He thus invokes a subversive "parade [where] the Deltas [must] unite and let their kinship defy the seas", to allow their mutual concerns of "pain" and their common experiences of "love and laughter" to power them to liberation.[136]

At a town-hall gathering in Dublin, Ireland, in a speech at a protest event against fracking (hydraulic fracturing) and Shell's involvement, Bassey declared that the "struggle in the backwater of the Niger Delta echoes back in Ireland".[137] His environmentalism can be said to be invested in a twin vision that is "at once profoundly local and profoundly transnational",[138] deriving from a belief that the struggles of the common people, especially in the Global South and the postcolony, have become the kernel that connects climes and peoples around the world at this moment in history.

Bassey's project of environmental rights activism through poetry is a strategic political and cultural critique of petrocultures in the oil sites. It is also an art of eco-protest, one in which he seems to build on existing modes of postcolonial ecocriticism to produce a subgenre of environmental justice literature. Huggan and Tiffin make a case for postcolonial ecocriticism while engaging with the work of the American ecocritic and philosopher, Lawrence Buell. Drawing on Buell's notion of "environmental imagination", that "engages a set of aesthetic preferences for ecocriticism which is not necessarily restricted to environmental realism or nature writing",[139] they insist that eco/environmental criticism needs to be understood as a "particular way of reading rather than a specific corpus of literary and other texts". They observe that ecology in literary criticism,

> [T]ends to function more as aesthetics than as methodology in eco/environmental criticism, providing the literary-minded critic with a storehouse of individual and collective metaphors through which the socially transformative workings of the environmental imagination can be mobilised and performed.[140]

My point is less to engage Buell's claims than to push Huggan and Tiffin's argument a little further. They suggest that while postcolonial ecocriticism performs an advocacy function, it also "preserves the aesthetic function of the literary text while drawing attention to its social and political usefulness, [that is] its capacity to set out symbolic guidelines for the material transformation of the world".[141] This is where their point becomes pertinent to Bassey's poetry of environmental and social justice advocacy. His poetry does offer a way of reading nature and a glimpse into how nature is conceived in the Niger Delta. Bassey's poetics of "Mother Earth" configures a transnational alliance against fossil fuel extraction. This alliance is premised on a certain ontological ethic that pairs environmental wellbeing with local praxis economics. In other words, Bassey does not repudiate the utilitarian relevance of nature to local indigenous communities that must live off their environment. Thus, through politics of advocacy performed in poetry, a compelling critique of petromodernity on a transnational scale emerges. This poetic form is able to capture and engage the often-elided aspects of environmental damage to local communities in a way that a purely environmental writing or political advocacy cannot achieve.

Conclusion

In these texts, we encounter how the earlier poets conceive nature as an entity that constitutes a regime of power under which the human subject exists. In relation to the awesome power of nature, human subjectivity is seen to be profoundly curtailed and in need of emancipation. I argue that this epistemological impression about nature features as a marker of a contradictory and paradoxical relationship between human subject and nature. It also, in a sense, provides an opportune text for petro-incursion, which tends to substantiate the logic of petromodernity as advancement towards development and modern civilisation. While it may be reasonable to state that the belief in modernity's promise of progress and development was not an unfounded one, it failed to provide the necessary (elusive) good life for those who inhabit this space. This failure stems from that continuous contest in which power struggles get caught up in much of contemporary modern life, where the promise and the real experience of happiness never really square up. In the depiction of temporality and environmental concerns that attend the incursion of oil modernity in the Delta, I argue that petrocapitalism manifests itself as a third category in the human–nature relation, to constitute a tripartite relationship. This incursion threatens the force and influence of nature in the affairs of humanity. But it also does not favour humanity (the autochthonous people). Petromodernity seems to make an inroad into the landscape with its own set of rules and practices, which do not derive from humans' innate quest for progress, modernisation and development but from singularly capitalist motives: to exploit and make profit. In the next chapter, I investigate the ways that this contest of power features in the form of neoliberalism and the logics of technological development, and within which petromodernity operates in the Niger Delta. In my reading of the poetry collections, I suggest that the poets reveal certain ways in which petromodernity intrudes on the quotidian, on the very mode of being in the Delta, to evolve its own cultural and social regime of operation – one that is different from that which exists between nature and human subjects.

2 People, fire and the Promethean allegory in the Niger Delta: Inversions in Ogaga Ifowodo's The Oil Lamp

In this chapter I use two figurations of fire in Ogaga Ifowodo's poetry collection *The Oil Lamp* (2005) to think through notions of truth and environmental justice as these bear out in the Niger Delta. The poems in this collection are quasi-historical and addressed to extractive capitalism's social and environmental upheavals in the Niger Delta in the 1990s. The poet employs metaphor and terrible humour to track and vivify the ways in which circuits of extraction inscribe fire's destructiveness in the petroleumscape of postcolonial Nigeria. Two figurations of fire emerge in the poems.

Firstly, fire tropes as material and vagrant, overindulgently destroying everything in its path – people and the environment. Secondly, fire figures as an object that operates beyond its physical aspects to signify the ugliness of unchecked power and corrupted democracy in Nigeria. Taken together, the poems studied here present fire as a natural element that has geopolitical significance. In a sense, Ifowodo's *The Oil Lamp* employs fire as a metaphor to depict the obduracy of power performed in the hands of a rogue postcolonial state. The poet draws on real events of the 1990s where military dictatorship and its attendant violence on the citizenry coincided with the apogee of Nigeria as the theatre of destructive oil extraction. Ifowodo engages these events as the twined context of postcolonial and neoliberal entanglements in the extraction sites of the Niger Delta. The form that fire signifies in Ifowodo's poetry is marked by oil spillages, state tyranny, petrofire and the infernal destruction of all that exists in its path. The trauma of witnessing petroviolence and injustice compels the poet to valorise felt experience over objectivity in giving account of the oil phenomenon. The Niger Delta is a landscape in which an insidious form of globalism operates within the oil industry.

In this chapter I draw on the Greek allegory of Prometheus for its conceptual framing. In the Greek legend, the story of Prometheus narrates into Western epistemology the ideals of human freedom and justice, taken for granted as universal propositions. However, I argue that these ideals are not necessarily universal in the manner of their distillations in postcolonial Nigeria. The otherwise emancipatory force of metaphoric fire inverses to signify as an accomplice of the destructive aspects of neoliberal extraction and its exactions on local communities.

Ogaga and his generation of writers

Ogaga Ifowodo is a Nigerian lawyer and poet who belongs in the era often described, in various formulations, as Nigeria's Third Generation Writers.[142] Harry Garuba's edited poetry collection, *Voices from the Fringe* (1989), is one of the earliest propaedeutic texts that signalled the relatively recent "emergence of a new generation of Nigerian writers", starting in the late 1980s and continuing up to the present.[143] This generation of writers includes such poets as Sesan Ajayi, Afam Akeh, Obi Nwakanma, Uche Nduka, Nduka Otiono, Onookome Okome, Remi Raji, Amatoritsero Ede and Ogaga Ifowodo. These writers are known for their intentionally provocative tenor intended to draw attention not only to themselves, young and impetuous as they were, but also to put under spotlight the overwhelming social and ecological deprivations suffered by the citizenry, the denial of basic human rights, and the fate of the postcolonial nation under corrupt military regimes. The lawlessness of the military was matched only by their extreme brutality towards any citizen who dared to challenge their absolute grip on power and apparent invincibility, which was shored up by the immense wealth of the oil in the Niger Delta. The denunciation of the military regimes brought these writers in direct confrontation with the despots, leading to their incarceration. Ogaga Ifowodo is one such writer, arrested and held in solitary confinement between 1997 and 1998 by the Sani Abacha junta because of his human rights activism and dissident writing.

Writing on the poetry of this era – the military dictatorships of the 1990s – Sule Egya says the poetry is so politically charged and socially engaging that it becomes "embedded in the historicity and culture that form the condition of possibility for its production".[144] Egya theorises this generation of poets more directly beyond the category of "generation", substituting in its place what he calls the "military era poets".[145] Indeed, the writing of this era engages and performs "a sickened context of nationalism",[146] where military dictatorship and its attendant violence on the citizenry coincided with the apogee of Nigeria as the theatre of destructive oil extraction. Ifowodo's *The Oil Lamp* engages this twin context of postcolonial and neoliberal entanglements in the extraction sites of the Niger Delta. The collection, published during the poet's postgraduate studies in the USA, demonstrates his sharp moral compass using fire as its organising trope to signify the violence of resource extraction.

Fire metaphor and the Promethean analogy

Fire in its various distillations has a long genealogy going back to classical Greece. Possessing material and symbolic qualities, fire embeds in the myths and legends by which the ideals of enlightenment and emancipation articulate and bear out in the social world. As a material element, fire exerts the power to transform whatever it meets; it at once burns and purifies. In its symbolic aspect, fire signifies as illuminating, and has the utility of a catalytic spark that brings about transmutation in substance or transfiguration in effect on the entity on which (or on whom) it is invoked. It can become accessorial to emancipation and education, revealing something that otherwise is not apparent. Take, for instance, the figurations of fire in classical Greek legend of Prometheus. In the Promethean legend fire features as a utility deployed to bring succour to humanity's "bare life",[147] and to create out of that bare life immense possibilities that would transform an otherwise banal existence into an extraordinary one ruled by human freedom, enlightenment and justice. Prometheus stole fire from the gods and gave it to mortals on earth, the people of Tartus, imbuing them with agency and subjectivity that enable them to determine their own fate and conditions of existence.[148] By this heroic act, Prometheus – who himself had godlike powers, but tempered by human instincts – helped to free the people of Tartus from the whims of outside forces and the tyranny of the so-called divine. He was, of course, punished by the gods and expelled from their midst. However, his heroism helped to unleash a series of events that led to the severance of the human condition from the vagaries of their tyrannical gods. In the process, Prometheus helped to inspire into existence a human community ruled by their own sheer will and emancipatory logic. Here we see fire featuring as a symbolic witness to an occasion of transformation and serving as an active agent in a transformational process.

Furthermore, fire features in literary depictions as a means of enlivening experience and inhabiting the possibilities of the imagination. Northrop Frye says that as a literary device, fire is inseparable from the ken of human experience, "already linked by analogy and identity with a dozen other aspects of experience. Its heat is analogous to the internal heat we feel as warm-blooded animals; its flickering movement is analogous to vitality; …its transforming power is analogous to purgation".[149] Frye's reflection here is in the Preface to The Psychoanalysis of Fire (1964), a text by the twentieth-century French philosopher and literary critic Gaston Bachelard. Bachelard on his part understands fire as "complexes",[150] that both catalyse and accompany human experiences and the way we think about the world – including our place in it. For instance, the child's unconscious processes of emancipation from parental authority can be illustrated using the fire analogy. Drawing on Freudian and Jungian psychoanalysis, Bachelard claims that children experience fire as both forbidden and irresistible. The child is forbidden from playing with fire by the parents; this simultaneously sparks the child's curiosity to push parental boundaries and explore further the possibilities of fire. This, of course, results in the child's disobedience and ultimate epiphany. Thus, fire becomes both material and metaphoric for the child's drives and her unconscious will to gain autonomy and knowledge.

If, in psychoanalytic understanding, fire accompanies growth processes by which humans come to a particular awareness and knowledge, fire articulates in ecocriticism as a materially apprehensible environmental agent. In their edited book Elemental Ecocriticism (2015), Jeffrey Cohen and Lowell Duckert explore the agential dimensions of the elements of nature – water, air, earth and fire – as a means to "think ecology and nature anew".[151] The book attempts a "dis-anthropocentric re-envisioning" of ecocriticism in which "thinking the limits of the human" conjoins with "thinking elemental activity and environmental justice".[152] Throughout the book fire is theorised as an elemental object that precedes humanity; humanity in turn mediates fire's utility for "transformation and change";[153] however, fire's agency is not *a priori* to human experience, its use value is at humanity's behest. Fire becomes the only element used exclusively by humans as living beings; other elements share their usefulness or agential significations with other life forms, plants and animals.

In sub-Saharan Africa, fire indexes vitality and abundance. This explains why "the hearth" tropes generatively in postcolonial African literature as the centrepiece of domestic life and a space from which critical agency develops.[154] In African music, fire foregrounds as something vibrant and energetic. Such is the example of the late legendary Afrobeat musician Fela Kuti, who sings of fire allegorically as emancipatory and agential, manifesting, for instance, in "the fire dance" that inhabits the "modern African woman", as we hear in Fela's famous song, "Lady". Moreover, beyond Fela Kuti's creative genius and onstage theatrics, this metaphoric fire is axiomatic also in the agency of his performing "Queens", twenty-seven of whom he famously married in the 1970s. The women would become a vital part of his successful band and a main repertoire of his performances in the 1970s and 80s.[155] Fire is thus a master-signifier, structuring the entire domain of experience and invigorating the processes of change, transformation, and human meaning.

Vagrant fire as the figuration of neoliberalism's vagrant power

These concepts of fire come under scrutiny, at once vivified and inverted, in Ogaga Ifowodo's *The Oil Lamp*. The poems in the collection are conceived in epic form, foregrounding three fire-related historical events – environmental disasters and socio-political upheavals that ensued in the Niger Delta in the 1990s:

- The 1995 extrajudicial murder of the writer and environmental activist Ken Saro-Wiwa and his eight Ogoni compatriots during the military junta of General Sani Abacha;
- The 1998 fire disaster in Jesse,[156] a riverside town in Western Niger Delta, that killed over a thousand people as they scrambled for petrol that was running out of burst pipes;
- The 1999 extra-judicial order by the federal government of General Olusegun Obasanjo to sack the town of Odi in South Eastern Niger Delta, where residents were accused of murdering some soldiers guarding the oil installation in the community.

Ifowodo tropes on these events, to memorialise their truth-value as a means of testifying to the abuse of power and the hollow democracy abetted by the free market enterprise of oil extraction in the Niger Delta. Ifowodo's collection of poems embeds the zeitgeist of this era, consisting of six parts that capture the times, namely "Jese"; "Odi"; "Ogoni"; "The Pipe War"; "Cesspit of the Niger Area"; and "The Agonist", dedicated to Ken Saro Wiwa and the Ogoni Eight. The theme of fire and its accessories of burning, destruction, purgation and truth-telling remain strong throughout the text.

Using fire as metonymic of destructive extraction, the poet brings to the fore the intractable operations of violence that exist alongside the various dimensions of oil production in the Niger Delta. One of the vectors by which to account for fire as metonymy is the interminable gas flaring that light up the rural skies of the Niger Delta, and discharge methane gas into the air. As Ike Okonta and Oronto Douglas, writing on the activities of Shell BP, note, "the obnoxious practice of gas flaring and oil leakages of Shell's rusty and corroded pipes"[157] are the physical evidence of their callous environmental policies in Nigeria. In other words, the technology of gas flaring is just a part of modernity's incursion into this landscape, inscribing all that is antithetical to progress and development in the region. Where technological advances enabled by fossil fuel have brought about material development and a semblance of progress elsewhere, the reverse is the case in the Niger Delta. With its landscape degraded and denuded, the Niger Delta is the embodiment of what Canadian writer Naomi Klein calls "Sacrifice Zones",[158] whose people and landscapes represent the collateral damage of petromodernity's onward march.

If oil is a product of "human scientific and technological inquisition",[159] extracting this resource has, alas, constituted the major source of underdevelopment and the collapse of cultural life in the provincial petroleumscape of the Niger Delta. Indeed, the politics of oil production continues to fuel the fire that engulfs, as it were, all forms of engagement staged by local communities in resistance to the ecological catastrophe. Various commissions of inquiry into oil explosions in the Niger Delta show fire to be a result of the same complexity as that which undergirds the production of oil in the first instance.[160] According to these reports, fire disasters in the Niger Delta are caused by both the oil industry and the violent methods employed by local communities to protest the injustices of extraction capitalism. Local communities employ methods that include illegal oil bunkering, artisanal refining of stolen oil, and the blowing up of pipelines by militant youth. These methods of protest are deplorable because they undercut the legitimacy of local concerns. At the same time, the traction they get in the media and other mainstream discourses leads invariably to easy distortions, such as sensationalism, which does nothing to mitigate the problems.

The 2013 Amnesty International Report reads in part: "Sabotage and theft of oil are serious problems in the Niger Delta", constituting, according to Shell, "75 per cent or more of the oil spilt" in the region.[161] Cajetan Iheka has rightly noted that the sabotage of oil operations by local communities through illegal bunkering and other subversive measures counterintuitively wreaks even more havoc to the life forms that inhabit the ecosystem.[162] However, the rhetorical strategy of describing the local bunkering as nefarious seems to me to let the oil multinationals off the hook. In a sense, such positioning, while offering a balanced and apposite assessment of the ecological crisis, can seem – if unintentionally – to place a heavy burden of proof on the local communities who often act out of desperation. The affected local communities lack the resources of scientific study to challenge the dominant views of local sabotage; they cannot afford the suave public relations to promote their cause, or expensive attorneys to defend their actions.

In the technologies of oil extraction in this region, fire accompanies the methane gas that expels from the pipes of drilled oil wells. In some other locations of oil production, the expelled gas is repurposed to some other usefulness, such as energy generation and domestic heating; this is not the case in the Niger Delta. Here gas is flared into the open sky, and burns to further pollute the air, while its viscous counterpart (crude oil) devastates the land. In this way, fire then indexes what crude oil signifies for the Nigerian nation: a promise and a curse;[163] its visibility on the horizon (as exemplified by the gas flares) does not seem to offer enough evidence to justify the urgent need for environmental restoration. In fact, it appears that its insidious devastation on the local environment is intangible and unconvincing, because it articulates alongside the more sensational fact of local sabotage and illegal oil bunkering. The impact of fire in this region is so pervasive it becomes difficult to identify without the risk of simplifications. Fire thus signifies the peculiar nature of oil's highly technical conduit that lies beneath the earth, unseen, extracted and piped away to produce development and prosperity elsewhere. As will be shown in the reading of Ifowodo's poems, fire's devastation in the Niger Delta is largely uninvestigated and its cause unproven; the useful instruments of science and legality necessary for proving are either unavailable or, where available, a travesty. I argue that Ifowodo's poetry bridges this very gap in the perspective of the local poor, whose everyday existence is riven in ways unaccounted for by the abstractions and detachments of scientific reports.

Building, therefore, on the above formulations of fire, I propose a postcolonial elemental ecocriticism that tracks the figurations of fire (as both agential and accessorial) into the petroleumscape of the Niger Delta. Reading Ogaga Ifowodo's *The Oil Lamp*, fire exceeds its physical signification, bringing into relief the "tension between metaphor and materiality",[164] while witnessing to extractive capitalism's social and environmental fault lines. Ifowodo tropes on fire metaphor of terrible humour and grotesquery, to track and vivify how the circuits of oil extraction operate within a postcolonial condition marked by infernal violence in the Niger Delta. Postcolonial ecocritical studies of Ifowodo's poems in this collection have favoured how the poetic voice articulates "the injustices of neoliberal globalization",[165] in which "issues of ecology are tied up with the struggles of people to survive in a heavily militarized environment".[166] I draw on these interesting studies to propose another direction of inquiry that focuses on the particular metaphor with which Ifowodo's poetry distils its postcolonial environmentalism – fire. I argue that the fire metaphor preponderates throughout the poems so powerfully, it becomes agential in its own right. In other words, while fire is itself a natural element, it is, however, by no means neutral in how it bears witness to the social and environmental deprivations in the region. Fire burns through the poems to produce a sobering truth about the true cost of oil extraction. Indeed, fire is accessorial to extractive capitalism's free market forces and the paradoxical "acts" of community protest that, together, produce tremendous ecological destruction and death.

The first figuration of fire that one gleans in the collection is in the poem "Jese", a fictional recount of the tragic events of the 1998 Jesse community fire disaster. Fire is shown in this poem to be material and vagrant, overindulgently burning its victims and destroying everything in its path, people and the physical environment.

> A rumour, said the wild music of deprivation,
> deaf to words unable to light stoves and lamps.
> The scramble went on, till the riot police came
> and shooting to disperse the frenzied crowd
> blazed the fiery trail of law and order.
> That was Odiri's tale of the cause of the fire
> moaned from a bed in the local clinic,
> whose calico sheets, gummed to her bum.[167]

The quoted lines open with the phrase "A rumour". This phrase operates to put pressure on the notion of truth, especially given the controversy that surrounded the explosion and the conspiracy theories that followed in the wake of the event, including the manner of its reportage in the media. In fact, the international media was especially unsympathetic in their coverage of this tragic event. See for instance the report by the BBC's Hilary Anderson:

> Hundreds of people have been burned to death in southern Nigeria after a ruptured fuel pipeline caught fire. Local newspaper said many of the victims were trying to collect leaking petrol when the explosion occurred near the oil-producing town of Warri. Several of the corpses were found still clutching plastic cups, funnels and cans they had been using to try to scoop up the fuel. The military state administrator, Walter Feghabo, has ordered a mass burial. There is no official word on what caused the fire, but correspondents say it is thought to have been caused by a spark from either a cigarette or a motorbike engine. The state-owned Pipeline and Product Marketing Company (PPMC) operating the pipeline has said the fuel leak was caused by sabotage.[168]

The reaction by Tony Jupiter, the country director of the environmental group Friends of the Earth, is a good counterpoint to that of Anderson:

> This tragedy underlines how the oil companies and Nigeria's corrupt government have put screwing as much money as possible out of the oil industry before public safety. The fact that people are scrambling in the streets to collect fuel from a burst pipeline shows how Nigeria's awesome oil riches are still being controlled by a few, rather than benefiting the many.[169]

In the reported incident, there is no mention of the devastation done to the environment in the spillage: the farmlands destroyed and the freshwater ways of the

Ethiope River into which the petrol flowed, polluting, and rendering it uninhabitable for aquatic life.

Ifowodo's poem troubles the dominant reportage by utilising unverified and unverifiable evidence given by the victims of the fire disaster, weaving out of these competing narratives the pitiable conditions under which local communities must subsist. The poem is filled with material textures of fire and its valances in the actual blaze as a testament to suffering that must speak, to tell its own – if inconvenient – truth. In re-enacting the sordid events surrounding the fire disaster, the poem memorialises the truth-value of lived experience as a means to testify to the forms of violence that capitalist notions of development inflict on the locale of energy resource extraction. The poem stages how localities such as Jesse community do not – cannot – fit into the seductive narrative of progress and prosperity that the economic model of neoliberalism promises. This provincial landscape does not fit into the logic of progress, which is why the "wild music of deprivation" is "deaf to" the promissory "words unable to light stoves and lamp".[170]

The concept of truth that the poem evokes, using fire as trope, proceeds from the memory of this historical event. Ifowodo has deployed this poetic memorialising of the oil encounter as part of his social and ethical commitment to righting the wrongs, that is, the unfairness of the ersatz neoliberalism that undergirds oil extraction in the Niger Delta. Toni Morrison has similarly ascribed her writing as an act of remembering, whose aim is truth-telling of a peculiar order. In "The Site of Memory" Morrison reminds us that her art is essentially "autobiographical",[171] constructed out of the arc of collective suffering experienced in the historical encounters of slavery, racism and colonialism. This conscious act of narrative memorialising is an injunction to a writer, Morrison argues, "who belongs to any marginalized category" because that group has been "seldom invited to participate in the discourse even when we were its topic".[172]

I argue that this is the call that Ifowodo heeds in depicting how the event of fire has produced conflicting accounts through multiple voices referenced as "rumour". Of course, the rumour is not to be dismissed easily, for its evidence is borne by the victims of the fire; their perspectives paired against other positions that participate in the discourse. In a sense, the multiple voices complicate the discourse of extraction in this petroleumscape, possessing elements of truth that are otherwise not apparent. The accounts that bear witness to the fire infuse any logical or official version of the event with doubt, as gleaned from the unreliable testimony by one of the victims called Odiri:

> But what can we trust she saw? remembered?
> Her daughter lighting up the sky
> before a cloud swallowed her? The finger
> at the trigger? The keg falling from her head,
> its spilled contents burning a path to her feet?

Hear another tale of how the fire started:
a bus driver, dizzy with joy
of a week's hoard of petrol, struck
a reckless match for the celebration
cigarette — his last visit to a filling station
too far back to recall the "No Smoking"
caution.[173]

Invariably, these conflicting accounts in the poem operate to make nonsense of the official reportage. Through what Mikhail Bakhtin calls "carnival voices",[174] it projects into the discursive mix alternative possibilities of what might have caused the fire disaster. The poet's style of conjecturing as a means of witnessing to the event is not neutral, even if on the surface it seems ambivalent. Rather, this poetic style pushes against the boundaries of evidential facts in a way that unsettles their truth-value, while at the same time opening up a possibility where a different kind of truth, ethical truth, might take root. The poetic technique of weaving the factual with the speculative of carnival voices has a collective hold on the reader's sensibility. What we see throughout the Jese poem are unreliable witnesses, conjectural and conflicting accounts, which are generative in ways that unsettle and challenge our otherwise calcified sense of the logical. It suggests, counterintuitively, that it is not the broken pipe that is at issue, or people's defiance in risking their lives by helping themselves to the spilled petrol. In contrast, what is at issue is the government's unwillingness to transform crude oil into wealth that is accessible to citizens. The consequence is a sheer spectacle of the wretched, scavenging for survival, even under the spectre of fire and its potential destructiveness. It is this symptomatic and sobering note of moral truth that becomes the striking point for the reader who encounters the fire's event in the poem.

By imbuing the events of the fire with the conjectures of the victims on the streets, Ifowodo has demonstrated the "need for artist-activist to go to the voices of popular dissent to find grounding for hope and the way to a better future".[175] With the myriad anecdotal evidence and conflicting accounts that these street voices throw up, disembodied facts – synonymous with sensational media reporting – are exposed in their inherent weakness in the face of the extraordinary suffering. Ifowodo's imaginative projection of the inscribed truth does not seek "the factual" evidence; by contrast it seeks to articulate an ethical truth, which legitimises the sheer will of the locality to survive. Again, Morrison informs us that the crucial task for the artist whose craft is borne out of social and ethical commitment "is not the difference between fact and fiction, but the distinction between fact and truth. Because fact can exist without human intelligence, but truth cannot".[176] Truth is, thus, contingent upon human interpretation, stimulating the will to justice and healing. In attempts at giving substance to truth, Ifowodo has collocated his moral conviction with the facticity of the events, the combination of which pulls towards moral justice.

Here is another poignant account that invites the reader to reach for a new lexicon, a new realm of knowing that is appropriate to the experience of suffering:

> A sickened earth rusted the pipes
> and threw up the lie encased in the hollow metal.
> Four boys chasing rodents for the day's meal –
> while their mates in cities where the pipes end
> learnt their letters in song and rhyme – were first
> to find the fountain. The mist of gushing oil
> blinded them long before the blaze. Their screams
> summoned the village for the hot shower,
> the ritual bath before sacrifice.[177]

We have here a nonhuman agent, the earth, acting in tandem with the multiple human voices to stimulate the reader into thinking anew the postcolonial ecology of oil extraction in this petroluemscape, to generate a set of ethical principles appropriate to the environmental cataclysm before the reader's eye. In fact, nature is here inviting the reader to a conscious act of incredulity, questioning the science that accompanies petroleum extraction in this region and the environmental and social fault lines it wrought. If "a sickened earth rusted the pipes/ and threw up the lie encased in hollow metal",[178] why then should one believe completely the facticity of local human sabotage? That the earth revolts and rusts the pipes is an indication of nature exerting its own agency while participating in acts that challenge any totalising narrative that deigns to blame the explosion on the poor communities. For, in representing the blighted environment of Jesse community in the wake of oil extraction, Ifowodo depicts the earth as agential. In doing so, the poem has tended to "speak *as* environment rather than *for* the environment".[179] Here the resistance strategies of the human and nonhuman are symbiotically rooted in ethical complementarity by the act of truth-telling that indicts the authorities through suffering, rage, and resistance.

A further consideration of the material figuration of fire as gleaned from *The Oil Lamp*, and particularly the Jese poem, is the literalising of an otherwise allegorical connotation of fire into a material one. The poetic intention to literalise fire's symbolism emerges first in the opening pages of the collection by its initial allusion to Dante Alighieri's *Inferno*:

> I saw so many flocks of naked souls,
> all weeping miserably, and it seemed
> that they were ruled by different decrees...
> Above that plain of sand, distended flakes
> of fire showered down...
> The dance of wretched hands was never done;
> now here, now there, they tried to beat aside
> the fresh flames as they fell.[180]

This excerpt from Canto XIV of Dante's *Inferno* features as one of the epigraphs to this collection. The "Jese" poem echoes the above lines of Dante, which reference hell fire and collective suffering as both atonement and consequence of sin. However, in Ifowodo's text this allegorical representation of fire is inverted into a literal experience of actual burning, suffering and condemnation:

> They wakened
> from their nightmares to the greetings of fire
> shrieked across dismal doorways by a child
> demented by the deafening whoosh![181]

Here the metaphorical damnation and rain of fire on the sinners in Dante's hell is a literal one for the local people of Jesse, where the victims' attempts to stave off the fire are, in fact, futile. Ifowodo's reference to Dante therefore begs the question: what exactly is the "sin" of the fire victims of Jesse community? Is it illegally siphoning petrol from the government pipelines? Alternatively, might it be the "sin" committed by the sheer misfortune of their geographical location, that is, of being located in proximity to the internationally constituted infrastructure of crude extraction? Perhaps this explains why the fire victims are "marked by oil for double torment".[182]

In a sense, the allusion to Dante's fire signals a similarly impending apocalypse in the Niger Delta. Dante's *Inferno* becomes a useful eschatological referent deployed to depict the palpable catastrophic consequences of extraction. Here is a locality so blighted by oil it becomes impossible to think outside the frames of apocalypse. Fire then becomes accessorial to the forms of globalism in the oil sites, ones that operate in accordance with the tenets of neoliberalism's extraction drive to obliterate all life forms that challenge its right of access to fossil fuels. Indeed, oil gorges out of its hosting locality an internationally constituted infrastructure that functions as a no man's land, an enclaved circuit of global flow. This cartographic logic becomes indifferent to indigenous existence; devoid, that is, of local intrusions, and impervious to the ecological harm inflicted on the locality by its operations. By implication any demands of recompense from the contiguous local communities whose lives and livelihoods are imperilled by oil pollution cannot be directed at the oil industry, since the landscape in question is considered an uninhabited crude wasteland.

The language of the poem is indulgently light-hearted; its use of fire imagery is emotive, organised to impact on the reader in ways both generative and affective. This perhaps explains why the poet presents the horrors of the explosion with sickening imagery and onomatopoeic connotations of fire's destructiveness, the whooshing sound suggests hastened burn wrought by

> the sizzles of body
> fat melting to add oil to oil, the crackle
> of bones bursting alight, the gurgle
> in her throat.[183]

If the situation described were not tragic and sickening, it would be comical, given the language of its narration. The lines vivify in the mind's eye a scene of grotesquery that is overindulgent in its fixation on the body being consumed in the fire. The tone of the poem evokes a sense of jest directed not at the fire's victims, but at the reader; it provokes horror and discomfiture at the grotesque violence that oil extraction and modernity's consumer culture built on fossil fuel continue to inflict on provincial landscapes and peoples. Ifowodo is here representing the disaster "as primarily caused by an imperial process of oil extraction and distribution" wrought by "vampire-like modernity".[184] The intensity of the mood created by this vampiric event is further drawn out by the minutiae of the burning body, evoking a life-like scene in which the reader cannot ignore the mass suffering. While the physical agony of the burning victims is the major refrain in the poem, the poetic voice also describes the violence projected by the authorities meant to quench the flames. Hence, one of the victims "saw the raised arms and guns/ The crack of trigger on hammer, her daughter's/ cries, and the shrieks of the scavenging crowd".[185]

Again, the visceral imagery of fire ravaging the body and the sounds filling the moments of a woman, "Odiri", who witnesses the murder of her daughter, are as if the poet has frozen and deconstructed this scene of intense violence, presenting fire as the agential *actant* in this drama of gore.

> It was fire for Jese, ashes and scars for all…
> After the deafening *whoosh*! some ran for creeks
> and rivers, some jumped in water-wells,
> some rolled on the ground, and some beat themselves
> or were beaten with broken branches.[186]

By focusing on the corporeal body, Ifowodo locates the ecological discourse of oil extraction in the Niger Delta as a profound actuality of lived experience intertwined with the local environment. His cinematographic language describing how fire consumes the bodies in the inferno provides a euphemistic bent to the horrendous incident captured in the poem. The lines are graphic and filled with auditory imagery, demonstrating how literary devices can re-enact and intensify a real event. Indeed, there is a sense of restrained hilarity in the manner of the poet's foregrounding of the body. This language of hilarity is similar to what Bakhtin describes as "laughter through tears" in his analysis of grotesque realism in the work of the renaissance French writer Rabelais.[187]

According to Bakhtin, the grotesque is an instrument of social satire deployed to depict the true nature of something that otherwise can prove incomprehensible. Bakhtin notes that the essential "principle of grotesque realism is to degrade",[188] by which he means to lay something bare; to render banal all that appears lofty, noble, abstract, or manipulated and obfuscated about that thing, especially in a society that exists under the sign of authoritarian power. Bakhtin uses the concept of grotesque realism to show how the material body can be the site upon which power, specifically external power, performs its authority, and establishes its dominion over the vanquished. Thus, to reveal the operations of power is to trace its mappings on the body, to read for the manner of its corporeal scarification. In a similar way, I read Ifowodo's trope of the grotesque in the corporeality of local bodies as an attempt to lay bare the delusions about the oil resource being the midwife of progress for Nigeria. By focusing on the body, the poet has used grotesque imagery to show how fire, as a material accomplice of extraction, does the work of degrading life in profoundly material and visceral ways. The jest, identifiable in the language of the poem, works to shock and re-sensitise the reader. It spares the reader no detail of the consumed body and the manner of suffering as experienced by the victim at the site where modernity derives and extracts its fuel, its energy. Thus, the body becomes the canvas on which extractive neoliberalism scripts and articulates its dominion on provincial life, extending outwards into the realm of social meaning.

Fire as a metonym of postcolonial tyranny

The second figuration of fire in Ifowodo's *The Oil Lamp* presents fire as a referential foil for the unravelling of postcolonial Nigeria as a non-democratic state, especially when it comes to the governance of the oil resource. If fire exercises material agency in the "Jese" poem, as I have discussed above, it is more symbolic in the second poem "Odi". Fire figures beyond the physical to exercise both ethical and epistemological agency. Here it operates to unveil Nigeria as a quintessential nation suffering from "the resource curse". More specifically, fire operates in the Odi poem to reveal the nature of justice and the corrupted legality by which oil extraction takes place in the Delta. By way of a context, the poem narrativises an actual historical event that occurred in 1999, at the dawn of the return to democracy in Nigeria, after sixteen years of military dictatorship. The people of Odi, a town in the Niger Delta that hosts some of Nigeria's oil installations, had staged a civil protest to draw the attention of the newly democratically elected federal government to the continued absence of meaningful development in their area, and the persistent environmental hazards that oil extraction posed to their community. In the melee that ensued from the protest, *some* people (actual statistics in Nigeria is an oddity), including police officers and soldiers sent to restore order, were killed. In reaction, the federal government ordered in the army to teach the villagers "a little lesson", killing over five hundred persons – mostly women and children:

> A battalion of justice scorched its path
> to Odi, came to solve by war
> a case of homicide: five cops and four
> soldiers sent to break a youth revolt
> lay dead in the dark labyrinth of the Delta.[189]

In this poem, the poet deploys his training as a lawyer and human rights crusader, by featuring the concept of justice in Nigeria as his subject of poetic ridicule. The poem jibes at the cruelty of justice with ironic collocation of incompatible concepts, namely "battalion" and "justice". The fire imagery in the form of the verb "scorch" makes jest of the notion of justice that purports to derive from democratic principles and practice. This explains why accompanying this odd combination is a metonym of fire that "scorches" the path along which this militaristic justice must travel egregiously to enforce the might of the state on a beleaguered section of its citizenry. The diametrically opposed collocation of "battalion" and "justice" operates to shock the reader's sense of justice and to heighten their experience of the absurd, of what it means to live under the sign of the marginalised in the landscape of extraction. Here is a poetic encounter that suspends one's usual rational objectivity for a subjective response, evoking empathy for those on the receiving end of this outlandish justice.

Further along on the same page, the reader can see exactly why this egregious administration of justice must be accompanied by metonymic fire, its accessorial utility, because at the helm of government is:

> ...the president,
> ex-commando, false-star-general,
> summoned the governor of the province
> for his orders: "By noon tomorrow, find
> the murderers or prepare the grounds for my men".[190]

In alluding to military imagery *passim* in this poem, using such terms as "battalion", "ex-commando", "false-star general", "surrender", "enemy" and "boots", the poet foregrounds Nigeria's recent history of military brutality. These lexical items evoke the horrors of the military cruelty of the 1970s, 80s and 90s, of which General Sani Abacha, the ludicrous dark-goggled dictator, was the most notorious. In re-enacting this historical event of military adjudication of justice, the poem does not valorise the rebellion of the local community youth, nor does it disavow the government's reprisal violence. Rather, it proceeds to question the government's brutal sense of justice; it questions an elected democratic dispensation that has sworn to uphold the newly scripted constitution, and yet reasons militarily.

The note of sarcasm in the poem is deployed, not just as "tone" critical of unchecked power, but also as "a clash of perspectives"[191] whose moral vision is revealed in the obscenity of the feedback loop through which the cruelty of the federal state unveils and deconstructs itself. Thus, in response to the president's request to fish out the culprits, the local governor in whose region this mayhem occurred, says:

> I have searched every house twice night and day;
> ...
> I have let children cry unfed till they slept;
> I have combed every tree's head, burnt every
> fishhut, rowed all the creeks, and not found them
> ...Come, sir, at once for the arrest.[192]

As these lines suggest, in the exchange between the governor and the president in search of the culprits, fire becomes the instrument by which justice seeks to be enforced. However, this fire is employed in a roundabout way; it is incidental to the search for the form of justice that is appropriate to assuage the president's wrath. The "scorched" path of justice in the opening stanza has resulted in "comb[ing] every tree's head, burn[ing] every/ fishhut" in the closing stanzas on the same page,[193] suggesting that, in this administration of justice, none must be spared in the locality – environment and people.

What is at play in the poem, therefore, is the banality of cruelty that reflects the state and, in the process, deconstructs the crudeness of its mindset. I argue, following Egya, that the language deployed in texts such as this does the work of "ideological contestation".[194] The minutiae of everyday local abjection become also the substance of the real, performing the struggle through "verbal action".[195] While the poetic voice evidently appears ambivalent, as it does not seem to take sides with either of the feuding parties – the community of Odi, on the one hand, and the Nigerian government, on the other – the deployment of irony is suggestive of where the poet's interest lies: with moral justice that protects the weak. It is, therefore, pertinent to make a case for justice through the broadening of the moral imagination that the poem invites the reader to participate in. The notion of justice does not exist in and of itself; justice needs to translate humanely into actionable good. Moreover, for this to happen, the task of stimulating justice into action hangs on the shoulders of those who have access to power: the intelligentsia, activists and writers. Indeed, the latter have a special mandate to stimulate justice into bearing out its true meaning in the public will, and, in the process, fiercely defend the weak. Ifowodo has taken this task to heart in this long poem. By employing consciously spawned ironies, the poet creates lines that are arresting, with grim details of human suffering as oil's paradoxical encounter with Nigeria leaves in its trail an illusion of progress for the postcolonial state, while at the same time destroying a vulnerable segment of the nation.

Conclusion

The objective of this chapter has been to examine fire and the manner of its signification as agential in the drama of oil extraction in the Niger Delta, focusing on Ogaga Ifowodo's *The Oil Lamp*. Ifowodo employs metaphor to engage historical events in which fire or its valences inflict forms of violence on the local ecology. The poet scripts out of this historicity of fire's destructiveness an ethical truth that inflects and destabilises what Judith Butler terms "the hegemonic field of representation itself".[196] Ifowodo's poetry of fire's destructiveness in the petroleumscape of the Niger Delta is more gripping than news reportage or any rational public dialogue regarding the modalities of resistance. The poet foregrounds human suffering as inseparable from the blighted landscape, especially where such cataclysmic events do not find proper media coverage. His poetry thus signals an important and alternative way of engaging the geopolitical and ecological discourses of resource extraction in provincial locations.

In the depiction of fire as an agent of destruction, Ifowodo employs onomatopoeic language to great effect. The poetry collection is rich with ironic metaphors, producing a peculiarly dark humour that enables the reader to persevere through the excruciating experience of encountering fire's destructiveness. With visceral imagery, the poet inflects fire allegory as a useful way to understand the oil encounter in Nigeria as a wasted opportunity to unleash the ideals embedded in the analogical Promethean myth, which the possibilities of fire otherwise evoke. Ifowodo's poetic vision in this respect takes root in certain arbitrary, eclectic, hybrid and decentred form, which inheres in a work of art. What inspires his poetry is a complexity of place, an environment blighted by the resource curse whose continuing social and environmental fault lines exist in the complicated "terrain of the unresolved, [while] acknowledging incoherencies, contradictions and multiplicities without seeking the resolution and coherence that grand narrative provides".[197] Oil extraction in this bioregion brings along with it an economy of Manichean proportions; a landscape with prodigious oil reserves and overwhelming social and ecological deprivations; a site of neoliberal capitalism heralded by the ideals of democracy and free market, which do not translate into meaningful and generative wealth for all. Nor does oil extraction guarantee environmental and social justice for the local populace that exists in the landscape bearing the oil that feeds the "chain of ease"[198] promised by free market ideologies. The poems I have analysed in this chapter articulate this atmosphere of anomie, limited choices and the unresolvable. The Niger Delta is produced in Ifowodo's collection as an embodiment of the Promethean fire, a terrible destiny that evinces Nigeria's vaunted greatness and yet faltering nationhood, reeling under the false promises of progress and development on which neoliberalism thrives to ensure its unmitigated access to fossil fuels. If, in Western epistemology, the Promethean allegory embeds the longings of freedom, justice and other emancipatory ideals, Ifowodo's poetry shows that these ideals are not universal, and certainly not in the postcolonial context of the Niger Delta. In fact, the Promethean fire features profoundly in its inversion; its otherwise emancipatory fire signifies as an accomplice of neoliberal circuits of extraction. It produces an infernal chain that deprives and disavows all longings that gravitate towards freedom and justice for the provincial life that exists under the sign of oil.

3 Versifying the environment of the Niger Delta as a critique of nationalism

> Nationalism is not a political doctrine, nor a program. If you really wish your country to avoid regression, or at best halts and uncertainties, a rapid step must be taken from national consciousness to political and social consciousness.[199]

This chapter aims at teasing out some of the concrete ways in which the tryst with oil modernity, that is, a form of petrosociality with nature and human subjectivity, operates within a neoliberal framework to produce a deeply flawed nation state. In Tanure Ojaide's *Delta Blues & Home Songs* (1998) and Ibiwari Ikiriko's *Oily Tears of the Delta* (2000), this nation state is figured as fraught, rogue even, by the fact of its inordinate reliance on oil as the basis of its existence and sustenance. Each of the poets deploys tropes of the biographical to construct a subversive "poetics of personal involvement",[200] to draw attention to instances of social disorder and violence inflicted upon the Niger Delta and its local lifeworld. The chapter is organised thematically across two sections, one for each of the centres of power, Abuja and Port Harcourt.

Using autobiography as a means of engaging the political, Ojaide poeticises his personal story as an embedded narrative in the history of Nigeria's national (un) becoming and its troubled relationship with oil. By deploying the autobiographical mode of articulation as a critique of the political, Ojaide's poetry is constitutive of eco-regional articulation, where the ecological wellbeing of the local is shown to be undermined by the purported economic interest of the national. Ikiriko's historicity in *Oily Tears of the Delta* focuses on the geopolitical constitution of cartographies. The poetry depicts the ways in which cartography, in the material forms of signposts and marked boundaries, operates as a visible marker of how neoliberal globalisation establishes and operates oil enclaves in the Niger Delta. The physical infrastructure of oil extraction becomes the site of contested power, and for apprehending the kinds of agency elicited in the local subjects affected therein.

In his book, *How Mumbo-Jumbo Conquered the World* (2004), British writer Francis Wheen names history as an ambiguous term used to "mean no more than what occurs in the world, or the techniques for finding this out, but also the discipline that orders events and experiences into an evolutionary narrative".[201] It is within the process of this creative ordering of events that I locate the texts examined in this chapter. The slices of history that one encounters in these poetry collections read as counter-narratives staged to thwart the materiality of the real and of history that confront the poets' imaginative visions. The process of creatively ordering events seems pertinent to the writer burdened with the social duty to intervene in moments of socio-political upheavals. Such ethical tasks can sometimes compel a creative nuance in engaging with the subject of historiography, especially when approached from the angle of poetic writing. Lewis Nkosi's analysis of history in African narrative is similarly illuminating. He notes how writers have often "dramatized moments in history when events have seemed to loom larger than any individuals". African writers, Nkosi argues, have often sketched out a "whole cycle of a people's history" where blind spots are "filled in", and unclear aspects are "re-examined, paraphrased and mythologised".[202] Nkosi's discussion provides useful insights when considering poetry in the present context of oil in the Niger Delta. His discussion of history illuminates the ways in which poets in the Niger Delta deploy local myths, history, and facts to create narratives that capture and represent certain recent historical events in postcolonial Nigeria.

Autobiographical narrative of the Delta environment: Localism contra nationalism in Tanure Ojaide's Delta Blues & Home Songs

Born in the oil-rich but economically impoverished area of the Niger Delta in 1948, Tanure Ojaide was raised by his maternal grandmother in a riverine village. In an autobiographical essay "I Want to be an Oracle", Ojaide romanticises this period as "an age of innocence in a rural home in the Delta region of Nigeria [when] the old ways were still very vibrant".[203] He writes, "Every first-born male child [among the] Urhobo is traditionally [deemed] a priest".[204] Ojaide tells of how, in spite of his received Christian beliefs of Catholicism, he is made to serve as acolyte to the traditional priest in his native shrine, as Urhobo custom demands. This syncretic ethos would later afford him the advantage of straddling two civilisations – African and Western – which bear upon his creative *oeuvre*. As a prolific poet from the Niger Delta, he has become something of a socio-cultural priest – a minority and environmental awareness priest.

There is an inter-textual relationship between Ojaide's personal history and his creative vision – his poetry and the cultural history of the Delta that he reconstructs in this collection. Ojaide hints at this inter-textual resonance in his autobiographical essay, where he discusses his poetic vision and highlights the ways in which his cultural roots continue to serve as creative muse. Although this claim of bucolic inspiration may not be peculiar to Ojaide, given that writers often ascribe their creativity to some natal provenance, Ojaide narrates his personal story as an embedded narrative in the history of the Niger Delta and its relationship with oil extraction. I suggest that this personal/natal history is held up to critique the notion of nationhood, a nationhood that is imagined, brought into being, and sustained by the fact of oil in the Delta, the very basis of Nigeria's GNP.[205] Thus, Ojaide's autobiographical poetry on oil in the Delta can be framed as a critique of Nigeria's tottering nationhood constituted to undermine the very existence of indigenous cultural life and the local ecology of the Delta.

Uzoechi Nwagbara reads Ojaide's poetry as an "ideo-aesthetic" creation, deployed "as a kind of public duty" owed "to the Nigerian people, to expose, reconstruct and negate the actualities of environmental degradation in the Niger Delta region of Nigeria".[206] Nwagbara's point is consistent with how Ojaide creates an imaginative reconstruction of his childhood as a near utopian past to serve as model for the remediation of oil polluted Niger Delta. While his primary interest is with the Delta environment that has been destroyed or is under the threat of pollution from oil extraction, the poet does also inscribe a human dimension to his environmental concerns. Ojaide locates a primordial human relationship with the environment through the valorisation of his own biography within the narrative, suggesting that what is being done to the environment has corollary effects on the human population who inhabit this environment.

Ojaide's poetry can be situated within what critic Funsho Aiyejina calls the "Alter/ native tradition" of Nigerian poetry, whose writing infuses "new traditional[ism]" with other acquired traditions, to mark a significant shift from the previous generation.[207] Enmeshed in the cultural left and radical politics, the writers of this generation moved away from the use of obscurantist images associated with Anglo-European modernism and slavishly copied by most of the preceding generation of African writers, namely but by no means exclusively Christopher Okigbo and Wole Soyinka.[208] Ojaide's generation resorted rather to the use of native metaphors that were aimed as altering the subhuman conditions of the oppressed in the postcolonial African states. British postcolonial critic Stephanie Newell discusses the "Alter/ native" aesthetic in the poetry writing of this generation as one that "captures the political energy and tensions in contemporary West African literatures better than the term 'postcolonial'"[209] Newell observes that writers within this alternative tradition "encapsulate the tension of writing against the postcolonial regime in the context of colonial history; they represent the effort to be native without otherness", exemplifying the difficulty of asserting a politics of resistance and radicalism "without being reactionary or assimilated by the dominant power".[210]

Free of idiosyncratic language and arcane imagery, Ojaide's poetry is essentially about the Niger Delta environment in which he first experienced life. It is from this vernacular texture of lived experience that he uses his poetry to engage questions of the place of justice and the meaning of dignity for local inhabitants of the oil extraction sites. In the poem "When Green Was the Lingua Franca", the poet stages a captivating affirmation of ecological well-being in the Delta before the oil incursion:

> My childhood stretched
> one unbroken park,
> teeming with life.
> In the forest green was
> the lingua franca
> with many dialects.
> Everybody's favourite,
> water sparkled.[211]

Using the evocative image of "green", a colour associated with ecology and natural vegetation, the poet persona takes the reader into an idyllic world of his imagined childhood. Here, he conveys the centrality of the greenery to his rural existence. The Niger Delta, just like the larger Nigerian federation, is a linguistically heterogeneous society with some forty languages and over two hundred dialects. The practical language of inter-ethnic communication is pidgin, a colonial contact language developed around the coastal areas, where the Europeans first made inroads into the hinterlands. This colonial language consists of Portuguese, French and English idioms, although over time, and given British colonialism in this part of Africa, English has come to constitute the major substrate of the pidgin language. So, it is this linguistic image of a unifying idiom that the poet draws on to describe the aura of cultural and ecological equilibrium in the speaker's recollection of his childhood world of the river delta. We are not sure whether the persona's retrospection is nostalgia for the idyll or the once lived, but we can sense through the imagery the vividness of the recall that this setting was once beautiful and pristine, with healthy vegetation and a body of fresh water.

With this near utopian memory and geographic description of the Delta landscape, Ojaide draws our attention to the subtlety of his lived environmentalism, which makes no less a damning commentary on the degradation of the ecosystem wrought by oil pollution and extractive capitalism. The poem reimagines the past, while imbuing it with a subversive reality that contrasts with and questions the present reality. The following stanzas are a sharp juxtaposition to the Edenic picture painted in the stanza above:

> Then Shell broke the bond
> with quakes and a hell
> of flares. Stoking a hearth
> under God's very behind!
> ...
> I see victims of arson
> wherever my restless soles
> take me to bear witness.
> The Ethiope waterfront
> wiped out by prospectors –
> so many trees beheaded
> and streams mortally poisoned
> in the name of jobs and wealth![212]

In Ojaide's biographical narrative of environmentalism in the Delta, Shell is responsible for the despoliation of the environment. But, of course, the term "Shell" is used both literally and metaphorically here, to critique how the destructiveness of oil extraction wrought various forms of violence on all that oil comes in contact with – environment and peoples. Literally, "Shell" refers to the actual oil prospecting and extracting company, Shell BP, the largest multinational company in Nigeria, so complicit in the destruction of the Niger Delta that a mention of the name evokes horror and anger in the hearts of most who live there.

Nevertheless, Ojaide uses the name Shell metaphorically, to stage a critique against the neoliberal logic of development that petromodernity purports to bring to local communities. The environment of these communities, and their otherwise self-sufficient local economy, is severely strained and the cultures threatened, wiped clean to write a new way of being, one that allows the insidious practices of resource extraction to force upon communities the deceitful choice between paid jobs and ecological well-being. According to the poet, the intrusion of petromodernity into this river delta has broken the bonds between nature and culture, human and environment – and the result is anarchy, which leaves in its wake a landscape riven with "victims of arson", "restless soles", "trees beheaded" and rivers "mortally poisoned". What these lurid images evoke is apprehended by many elsewhere in the world as the apocalyptic future caused by anthropogenic climate change, the Anthropocene. However, in the Niger Delta, this seemingly abstract yet-to-be agreed-upon notion is already a quotidian reality, the very sociality of that blighted region.

If "When Green Was the Lingua Franca" is a subtle call for environmental justice, the poem "Delta Blues" is a dirge to the poet's natal land. Beginning with the title, this eponymous poem is a song of lamentation and protest poignantly rendered in a mood reminiscent of the anti-slavery negro spirituals in the African American literary tradition. The poet laments the upheaval caused in the ethical life of the communities, resulting in greed, violence, and death.

> This share of paradise, the Delta of my birth,
> reels from an immeasurable wound.
> Barrels of alchemical draughts flow
> from this hurt to the unquestioning world
> that lights up its life in a blind trust.
> The inheritance I sat on for centuries
> Now crushes my body and soul.[213]

What we have here is a narrative of intimate environmentalism. Ojaide uses first person pronouns such as "my", "I" and "me" and other lexical items, namely "my birth", "home", "my nativity", as markers of belonging to give authenticity to the testimony he bears. With a mournful cadence, the poet decries the violence of environmental despoliation visited upon the landscape by the so-called industrial development of the oil resource:

> My nativity gives immortal pain
> masked in barrels of oil –
> I stew in the womb of fortune.
> I live in the deathbed
> prepared by a cabal of brokers
> breaking the peace of centuries

> & tainting not only a thousand rivers,
> my lifeblood from the beginning,
> but scorching the air and soil.
> How many aborigines have been killed
> as their sacred soil was debauched
> by prospectors, money mongers?[214]

As the poet-persona recounts the plight of the marginalised, he also invokes an image of the vanishing vegetation, a landscape blighted by extractive capitalism. The Delta environment is starkly projected here as a hyper object of desire, a commodity that is reified, in fact, deified over its habitats.

Ojaide's testimony against petromodernity in the Delta soon crystallises from a personal narrative of autobiographical environmentalism into one of a local/communal eco-articulation. He embeds cultural history in a narrative of nature to stage a critique of the Niger Delta environment in the throes of petro-extraction onslaught. Perhaps this explains why, in the last three stanzas of the poem, Ojaide connects the devastation of the Niger Delta environmental to a physical violence inflicted by a hangman who performs state-sanctioned executions, in this case, of the Ogoni Nine, in reference to the execution of Saro-Wiwa and his colleagues. Implicit in this collection, therefore, is the perception of violence as a prevailing condition under which the oil industry is constituted: its effect on the environment is violent, just as any attempt to bring attention to this problem is met with a corresponding violence; an instance is the Ogoni saga. Charles Bodunde argues, "Ojaide interprets Saro-Wiwa's death within the wider contexts of political struggle and national tragedy", so that "Saro-Wiwa's case symbolises the aspirations and will of a community and the complexity of a political struggle".[215] This line of thought is further realised in the poem "Wails":

> I must raise the loud wail
> so that each will reflect his fate.
> Take care of your people,
> they are your proud assets.
> The boa thoughtlessly devours
> its own offspring, Nigeria's
> a boa-constrictor in the world map.[216]

Ojaide discovers in the courageous and irrepressible minority rights' leader useful folkloric armour against totalitarian regimes just as the elephant shields its young ones from the predator's rampage. Perhaps this explains his image of "the elephant"[217] to describe Saro-Wiwa as a hero who looms large in the minds of the people. It also calls to mind the fate of the elephant, once abundant in Africa and a symbol of Africa's pride and strength. However, elephant tusks fed the colonial criminal enterprise of ivory trade, which saw the death of many elephants. Today, the elephant is an endangered species on the African continent and, while the ivory trade has been restricted, elephants remain prey to illicit poaching. It is this concrete image of the endangered elephant Ojaide draws on to describe the death of Saro-Wiwa, a moral voice of truth and justice, symbolising the people's struggle against forms of oppression and exploitation. The final stanza is the climax of the poem:

> Streets echo with wails.
> A terrible thing has struck the land,
> everyone is covered with shame or sorrow –
> this death exceeds other deaths.
> They have murdered a favourite son,
> this news cannot be a hoax;
> for the love of terror,
> they have hanged a favourite son
> and eight other bearers of truth
> Nobody fools others about these deaths.[218]

Tayo Olafioye remarks that "Ojaide is able to transform the image of pain into artistic form because he is not only an artist but the voice of his people, more accurately, the Oracle of the Delta".[219] In the traditional setting of the Niger Delta and perhaps elsewhere, an oracle – the knower and seer of hidden things – was not only concerned with lamentations and condemnation of ills in the society, but also prescribed ways of addressing these ills by providing workable alternatives to mitigate the challenges that plagued society. Ojaide believes (and he states this quite emphatically) that "commemoration of all that is good in the past…is still viable… in the present [and] should inspire hope".[220]

Ojaide is an oracle not of doom but of hope. His poetic vision expresses a call for the restoration of a liveable environment in his homeland. He believes that, since he has been a witness to the good past, as he succinctly "versifies" in this collection, he knows what has been lost and can serve as a model for rebuilding the crumbling structures of the present. Hence, the poem is not all about grief and despondency. He provides a glimmer of hope in the image of renewal and continuity of the struggle, which is signified by the transfer of the mantle of leadership – of heroism – from one activist to another:

> After the warrior-chief's fall,
> somebody else will carry the standard—
> Boro left for Saro-Wiwa to take over,
> the stump will grow into another *iroko*.
> The hardwood shield is broken,
> the people are exposed to a storm of abuse;
> the diviner's spell is broken
> & everybody's left in the open.
> But the diviner's words are never halted
> by death – *Ominigbo* is my witness.[221]

The above poem, and in fact most of Ojaide's poems dedicated to the memory of Saro-Wiwa and his eight colleagues, evoke that time-tested African belief in the "life after death". This becomes a source of consolation that creates for the collective a new horizon of hope, one, I believe, that would sustain the struggle for justice and a regeneration of the environment. In a sense, this reinforces my earlier point about the poet as an oracle of good tidings and not one of doom, an unapologetic optimist.

Take for instance, the poem "Elegy for nine warriors", where Ojaide engages with this trope of life-after-life: a continuance of life even after the physical event of death. He portrays the "Ogoni Nine" as "warriors" who have become immortalised in the lore of sub-regional and ethnic cosmology, and etched into mythology by their bold attempt at confronting the might of the Nigerian state on behalf of the Niger Delta:

> Those I remember with these notes
> walk back erect from the stake.
> The hangman has made his case,
> delivered nine heads through the sunpost
> and sored his eyes from sleepless nights.
> The nine start their life after death
> as the street takes over their standard.[222]

Ojaide's passion for exploring traditional African folklore is undeniable. Writing in a tradition of abuse poetry modelled on the Urhobo *Udje* dance song of cursing and lampoon, Ojaide repudiates the notorious hangman responsible for the death of these folk heroes, whose blood will continue to whet the appetite for progressive dissension in the troubled region and in Nigeria. In this poem, Ojaide employs repetitive words for effectiveness and the advancement of the intensity of his message. The repeated use of "those I remember" reinforces the persona's homage to the Ogoni Nine and his unflinching support in the cause for which they died. The poem reads like a chant to herald "the nine" into the bliss of afterlife, so that their demise does not leave the people in a state of despair but charges them into action, to actualise the demands for which the leaders made the supreme sacrifice.

In the poem "Abuja" Ojaide frowns at the socio-economic imbalance that has generated political altercation and caused the Delta populace to live in abject poverty, a paradox of living in lack amidst plenty. The poet constructs a seditious narrative of geo-politics in Nigeria, demonstrating how the political foundation upon which the nation state exists (that is if one truly exists) stands revealed in its starkest weakness:

> Here where all cardinal points meet in a capital
> here where rocks raise homes to the sky
> here where the savannah rolls over the soil
> ...
> this is where range chickens consume and scatter leftovers
> this is where the hyena's den is guarded by rings of packs
> this is where the hyena cornered the hare
> and swallowed it, leaving no scent for a trace
> ...

> & laugh at the plight of a hundred million cowards
> this is where the national flag covers a cesspool
> this is where a god led his worshippers to die
> this is where I weep for my entire land.[223]

This is probably the more compelling poem in which Ojaide's poetics of locality as a scathing critique of nationalism is realised. The poem is a fast-paced narrative, a riveting rendition that dramatises the inherent material contradictions that the national wealth from the oil resource performs in the polity of national engendering in Nigeria. The poem gives a metaphoric resonance to what Ilan Stavans has called "an illness of abundance",[224] which orchestrates a combination of excess and opportunism that attracts a band of national leadership notorious for crassness and profligacy.

In the third chapter of *The Wretched of the Earth* (1961), Fanon provides a compelling diagnostic of the problem of national chauvinism and the crop of leaders that it produces in postcolonial Africa. Fanon considers this form of nationalism hollow, precisely because it is a nationalism lacking in social and political consciousness. It is a nationalism that is uninterested in any meaningful production, invention or building; but whose leadership is completely given to canalised activities of racketeering, to taking advantage of those aspects of the economy that generate easy money, such as oil, but that add no value to the lives of its people and bring no actual development to the nation. Fanon describes this class of national leadership as "stupidly, contemptibly, cynically bourgeoisie"[225] who alienate themselves in the cities and metropolises of the nascent nation.

Fanon concludes by enjoining postcolonial African leaders to redeem themselves by working to develop a political and social consciousness in which the dignity of the citizens is restored, humanism is deepened, and a "human landscape" is built for harmonious existence. By human landscape he means "The living expression of the nation" – not the brightly lit palaces "where sits the government", but a landscape characterised by "the moving consciousness of the whole of people"; especially in the countryside, for it creates "a prospect that is human because conscious and sovereign men (and women) dwell therein".[226] Alas! Fanon's is an admonition unheeded by Nigerian leaders. Thus, Abuja represents the very parochial nationalism that Fanon deplores – a fundamental weakness of nationalism, an issue Ojaide's poem engages with. Abuja is thus metonymic of the insular Nigerian leadership, the parochial ruling elites. The poem "Abuja" re-enacts and vivifies how the city embodies the insular wealth that oil generates. The oil wealth is available only to a small coterie of politicians, who, by the fact of living in Abuja, are geographically divorced from the harsh reality of the consequences of their misgovernance amongst the larger Nigerian population.

The poem also foregrounds how political power operates to alienate the populace from the gains of the natural resources, which providence, by virtue of their location, offers. The masses live in squalor, while the resources from their land build mansions elsewhere. The poem becomes a cry for the poet's homeland as it could have been, and against what should not be the scheme of things, at the seat of power, Abuja.[227] It signals a feeling of alienation and betrayal. Indeed, what we see is an alienation at once political, cultural and social; precisely because the local populace has been stripped of their land, the very means on which any modicum of existence depends, and which results in what Nixon describes as "displacement without moving".[228]

Nixon talks about the people's loss of the land and resources, a loss that leaves communities stranded in "a place stripped of the very characteristic that made it inhabitable".[229] The Niger Delta's peculiar geography compels a nature-dependent economy of fishing and farming. The exploration of oil and the resultant pollution of the wetlands and rivers have greatly affected this agrarian economy. Since the people are denied equitable access to the oil wealth, it stands to reason that they are doubly short-changed, which result in the "displacement without moving".

The repetition of "here" and "where" in the poem suggests locality, but this locality is undermined in each case by the rest of the phrase, which refers to a particular elsewhere, Abuja. Abuja signifies as the stage where the existence of oil in the national political process dramatises the paradoxical combination of extravagance and poverty of vision; it becomes a place where the nastiness of Nigeria's oil-driven nationalism is revealed. Tijan Sallah notes that "place conveys a deep sense of history".[230] Abuja conveys the historical weakness of Nigeria's fiscal federalism, one constituted to favour disproportionately the central government at the expense of other federating units. Every wealth generated in the regions, such as oil revenue in the Delta, is carted away in colonial-style, plundering the resources of annexed enclaves, to develop Abuja. Thus, Abuja becomes everything that the Niger Delta is not.

The questions of inequality and lopsided fiscal federalism in the Nigerian polity consistently hunt the lines of this deeply lyrical poem. The beauty of the lyricism is at odds with the narrative it projects: the disconnection between government and governed, between the origination of wealth and where it is amassed. The image of exploitation and depravity of the people that Abuja represents is discernible in the poet's continuous repetition of "this is where". Thus, the poem becomes a narrative of social and political exclusion, questioning the continued denial of a particular region of patrimony to the wealth that their homeland and physical landscape bears.

Ojaide's ability to measure the Deltascape within the gamut of his poesy is born out of his deep-rooted and sustained relation with the region. The unhappy shift as represented in the metaphor of a landscape falling into visible ruins can be traced to the absence of a vision in governance. This, according to the poet, is manifest in the ways in which unthinking and parochial rulers (not leaders) have shattered the people's hopes and usurped their means of livelihood. Ojaide's poetic oeuvre demonstrates a lived and imaginative cultural relationship with his homeland, which is scripted in the context of oil production. His poetic aesthetics and practice are lyrical, not grand. He refracts, through imaginative reconstructions of his birthplace and its delicate ecology, the precariousness of people's lives in the face of neoliberal capitalism and the global race for oil. Ojaide does not escape from the fact of the destructive extraction happening in his homeland, by recreating an idyllic world of his childhood environment. Rather, the poet invokes his childhood past as a way of contrasting it with the present, to draw attention to the social dissonance and environmental violence inflicted on the landscape as consequence of crude extraction and so-called national development. What we see in the disorder that the poetry depicts is the ramifications of this violence, not only for the delicate environment but also for the writer's poetic memory of his imagined past, of his natal relationship with the environment, and this compellingly holds the historical present in critical contrast and vilification.

Poetics of cartography: Globalism and the "oil enclave" in Ibiwari Ikiriko's Oily Tears of the Delta

Ibiwari Ikiriko was born in 1954 in Kano, a city in northern Nigeria, but he grew up in Okrika, an inner-city suburb of Port Harcourt – the largest city in the Niger Delta and the commercial capital of the petroleum industry in Nigeria. He unfortunately died soon after his first and only poetry collection, *Oily Tears of the Delta,* was published in 2000. Oyeniyi Okunoye notes that "In spite of his very short career as a poet, Ibiwari Ikiriko's work is probably the most representative of contemporary Niger Delta poetry in the sense that it primarily articulates a regional consciousness".[231] This regional consciousness in Ikiriko's poetry consists of cartographic and geopolitical tropes with which he engages oil extraction and the tenets of globalism that govern it in the Niger Delta. If Tanure Ojaide's poems begin on a nostalgic, autobiographical note, the poems in Ikiriko's collection invite the reader to think of cartography, in the form of signposts and boundaries, as providing visible markers of the ways in which neoliberal globalisation establishes and operates oil enclaves in the Niger Delta. The poet engages these infrastructures as sites of understanding power and the kinds of agency that are enabled or, indeed, are stifled in places where oil is extracted to feed global consumption.

Oily Tears orchestrates a crosscurrent of voices competing to be heard, calling attention to themselves in insurrectionary enactments of geopolitical articulations and the performance of a regional identity. In considering the poetics of cartography that Ikiriko articulates in this collection, my reading is therefore based on the assumption that there is an expressive impulse of a socially charged interaction in the text. It expresses, following literary theorist Mikhail Bakhtin, certain "dialogised interaction"[232] with meaning-bearing signs and power-enforcing symbols that circulate in the local sites of the oil installations. The signs are put up by the government in conjunction with the oil multinationals, to indicate the right of way for the oil pipelines underground, but these signposts actually inscribe images that suggest possession of the land on which they stand. In my discussion of Ikiriko's *Oily Tears* I show how his poetry addresses these signposts by deconstructing the forms of power and control they perform in the public spaces of habitation in the Niger Delta. The poet thus troubles and re-appropriates these inscriptions, to place their true significance in stark relief.

Bakhtin's notions of the social event of speech interaction and heteroglossia allow one to unpack the expressive impulses of Ikiriko in this poetry, particularly the ways in which he uses language as an instrument of mediation between the text and contexts, to project a form of dialogised interaction. Although Bakhtin is well known as a major theorist in novelistic discourse (he argues, for instance, for dialogism as a particular kind of novelistic discourse), his ideas of social heteroglossia are well suited to understanding Ikiriko's poetry. In "Literary Stylistics: The Construction of the Utterance", Bakhtin explains how language is constitutive of the social space within which it functions as a continually evolving category:

> Language is most certainly not a dead, frozen product of social life: it
> is in constant flux, its development following that of *social life*. This
> forward movement in language is realised in the process of human
> communication not only in connection with production, but also in the
> course of speech communication…Speech communication…is no more
> than one among the many forms in the development (coming-to-be) of
> the social group in which speech interaction takes place between people
> participating in social life. Hence it would be a futile waste of effort to try
> to understand the construction of utterances, which make up the element
> of discourse, without any reference to the actual social environment
> (situation) which has evoked them. [T]he true essence of language is the
> social event of speech interaction, manifest by one or several utterances.[233]

Bakhtin argues that all forms of utterances are constitutive and derivative of an inherently "sociological character of the human consciousness [of] experiences and their expressions".[234]

Bakhtin describes the term "heteroglossia"[235] as deriving from the word heterogeneous, which means socially diverse and linguistic multiplicity of being, in this case, the presence of voices. The sociality of these voices undergirds their ability to deploy language as an interactive tool of exchange through dialogue. Heteroglossia is therefore the social texture that gives concrete expression to discourse and meaning to social consciousness, the multiple voices calling attention to ideological standpoints. What I draw from Bakhtin's concept of social heteroglossia is the primacy of language as the connection between text and context – language is the mediating agent by which interaction between text and reader is organised and performed. Indeed, Ikiriko's poetry finds expression in Bakhtin's notion of heteroglossia, in the sense that it feeds from, and engages, the public domain of quotidian sociality in the Niger Delta, a sociality conceived in its real, material textures.

The site of oil extraction, the Niger Delta, is rendered a heteroglot space in Ikiriko's collection. Beginning with the first poem, "Evening Already", there appears to be an enactment of a certain dialogic protocol that is taking place in the mind of the poet persona:

> I had listened
> To the voices within me
> To the voices around me
> That I am a time-bomb.
> Now I realise
> That I am only a landmine.
> I had listened
> To the voices within me
> To the voices around me
> That I am an oil bean seed
> Now I realise
> That I am only a coconut!
> I cannot detonate
> Without external pressure
> I cannot disperse
> Without external agency.[236]

We notice that the persona seems to be engaged in a soliloquy, dialoguing within, as well as between, the self and an ostensibly material event of social discourse symbolised in "the voices around me" over what later emerges as "cares", a recurring referent throughout the poem, with which the persona explores a number of concerns that irritate his sensibilities. The persona breaks into a dramatic monologue, as though he has been contemplating these concerns for a while. We do not quite know why he is getting impatient and pressed for time, as we glean from the urgency of tone:

> And before me
> I see day's light
> Changing from gold
> Past silver,
> With shadows lengthening.
> Yet I am resolved
> Not to be wasted by time
> And I know why I live
> To say these things are still to do.
> Cares.
> Clamping weight of cares.[237]

The reader hears the webbed words, echoing in the mind's ear, of one possessed with the muse to excoriate, yet burdened by the concerns he speaks about. The persona seems to scorn at his indulgence in waiting patiently at a cost he can no longer afford. We are only introduced to what his complaints are about in the second stanza of the poem. He seems to imagine himself as embodying a personified subject of a geographical landscape, and as such, he is no longer willing to bear the burden of external agency, one that exploits the persona's hospitality, a sacrifice that amounts to nothing:

> Cares crowd around me
> Like wretched huts around
> An only Queen House
> On a land-starved island
> Fed upon by the encroaching sea
> That offers difficult terrain excuses
> For majority policies to keep it so
> Enshrouded Beauty failing to exude.
> I am immersed in cares
> Like a cock in crude oil,
> Jugular glutted, glottis jaded.
> Time crier belated.[238]

Here his engagement with the politics of enclaving and offshoring surfaces for the first time. He calls the Delta a "land-starved island" fed upon by externalities, which he describes as an "encroaching sea" that gives unconvincing reasons of "difficult terrain" for not developing the hosting entity, the Delta – an area that bears the wealth for the nation. Although situated within a specific locale of the Niger Delta, the poem (and perhaps the entire collection) activates a dialogue with the global by addressing itself to this oil industry situated in that locality. His narrative stages a dissident act, which performs his ethnic identity, to undermine the placeless ethos of the oil infrastructure. The continuous allusion to the geography of the Niger Delta and its cartography as one that is locked or trapped within the territorial operations of oil extraction make the images read not as metaphors but as material referents.

Ikiriko's poetry performs an interrogatory act against the signposts that communicate certain ideology-embedded messages and authorising instructions in the spaces of oil installations. One encounters these inscriptions and the boundaries they mark off as forms of intrusion that not only legitimise the activities of resource extraction by the multinational corporations, but also disavow local subjectivity in at least two ways. On the one hand, they reinforce notions of the Niger Delta as a quintessential oil site that is heterogeneous, international and readily available for the exploitation of its oil resources. On the other hand, they legitimise the national government's actions and inactions in the Niger Delta. Thus, the poet undertakes to re-appropriate these local signposts and meaning-bearing images that, to him, hold a powerful influence on the psyche of the local populace, invoking them to function as "dialogizing backgrounds"[239] to his poetry.

The above point is illustrated in the poem "Under Pressure", where Ikiriko conjures up signs, symbols and images to challenge the mechanisms of power at work in the environment of oil extraction, especially the oil-transporting pipelines that populate the region. The poet questions how these signs and images operate to control and contain local communities in their everyday lives:

> DANGER!
> High pressure oil pipeline – keep off!
> Don't anchor!
> DEATH!
> High tension gas pipeline – keep clear!
> No fishing!
> WARNING!
> High pressure pipes – keep away!
> No berthing![240]

The poem articulates a particular process of systematic intrusion that the signposts perform in the Niger Delta. At least three levels of this intrusion may be construed, and they all operate to alienate the human population from the oil ecology of the Niger Delta. The first identifiable level is that of the physical, spatial intrusion. This impedes and destabilises the very physical space of human existence. It operates to govern local agency, in that it restricts human presence and freedom. It inscribes and constitutes for itself, within itself, a spatial demarcation, a form of physical segregation between the oil resource and the local population. This distinction is delineated by the announcement of the physical presence of the pipelines. Even when the pipelines are underground, the inscriptions announce their malicious presence through the signposts, by their instruction to the public to "keep off!" and steer clear. This form of intrusion operates to restrict the daily physical movement and mobility of the local populace. It dictates to the local human subjects where to venture and not to, how to move and loiter.

The second form of intrusion performed by the signposts orchestrates an economic, as well as a cultural, interruption. It meddles into, disrupts and controls the territorial economy. It declares: "DEATH!/ High tension gas pipeline – keep clear!"[241] This inscription decrees where, how and what daily vocations should be conducted. It forbids the local populace from their practice of maritime economy in the form of fishing, sailing, berthing and wharfing. The local communities are thus excluded from and denied their means of livelihood and survival, as the signposts warn them against berthing their sea-going vessels, while also threatening them with "DEATH" if they venture to fish in the waters. In fact, all essential preoccupations of the local communities, given the nature of the terrain, are suspended so that the global commodity of oil can be transported without hitch or hindrance to its point of consumption. The pipelines that crisscross the Delta, piping away the oil to other climes, are captured here as a societal menace, bent on wrecking the land and the people. While these pipes drain the natural resource from under the feet of the local populace, they also pose danger and frighten them, deterring them from going about their domestic businesses.

The third and final form of intrusion is one that operates at the psychic level. According to the inscription's signification:

> *Tresspassers* will be compressed.
> Roasted. Melted.
> O what a full tide of pressure
> Brim they over our land and persons.[242]

By announcing this deterrence against whose caution evisceration is probable, the inscriptions thus perform a kind of legitimate power with the right to inflict violence if necessary. This logic operates to powerful effect in the local communities where the oil infrastructure is sited. Indeed, having restricted human movements and alternative means of livelihood, this third level of intrusion banishes them from the landscape by declaring them "trespassers": a category of outsiders, invaders. This, in one sense, enforces a form of intrusion with a legal instrument that has a superior force to disarm, threaten and strip them of any claim to autochthony that would have served as the basis for resisting such psychological violence. Here is a manner of intrusion that operates effectively and dangerously within the tenets of neoliberalism. The writer and environmental activist Nnimmo Bassey notes that, in the protocol of capital's resource extraction, "Communities are dislocated from their material means of production, separated from their systems of sustainable livelihood and made to become bystanders on the dusty byways".[243]

I suggest that the choice of words, punctuation and even spelling in the poem functions to incite the reader to act in a manner that is resistant to injustice and oppression. The poem utilises a structure that brings into sharp focus the material texture of the oil's presence in the local communities. Thus, the words in block letters, followed by exclamation marks – "DANGER!", "DEATH!", "WARNING!" – and the wrong spelling of the word 'trespassers' are meant to evoke this manifestation. However, they also indicate an intention by the poet to stir up a particular reaction in the reader, an intentional provocation to (re)act against perceived threats of annihilation in the locality. Every word in the opening stanzas is made to account for itself and to point in the direction of a transgressive reaction that the poem and its analogous context of the signposts are meant to stoke. This incitation to transgress resonates with the realpolitik of the Niger Delta, a region where protests against the oil industry and the federal government are a daily political exercise. Moreover, while Ikiriko appears to be reticent about this imminent outcome, his choice of punctuation is suggestive of that possibility. Taken together, the poem functions, following Terry Eagleton, as "something which is done to us, not just said to us; the meaning of its words is closely bound up with the experience of them".[244]

In the poem "Devalued", the same streak of incitation is conveyed in a narrative that throws the conditions of violence, with all its historical and systematic valences, into clarifying relief:

> Our yesterdays
> Have been diluted

With debased deeds
Our todays, devalued
Are no more weighty
Than a dollar bill
And our tomorrows
Are mortgaged by
Home brokers to foreign clubs
So, finished we are
Unless we gather in concert
To break these brokers.[245]

The poem gives expression to some ethno-regional tensions that continue to define Nigeria's postcolonial history, particularly the issue of resource control – a knotty geopolitical contestation over fiscal federalism. Hence, the Niger Delta is figured to be the goose that lays the golden egg but is left to starve and denied a share in the wealth it produces, just because it lacks the political influence to sway state policies around oil governance in its favour. The poem conveys a rallying summons for the re-evaluation of such fiscal policies and reveals how the rights to equal citizenship within the larger Nigerian state are denied to the Niger Delta, portrayed as "Mini Minor Minority Man".[246] This perception emerges from a shared sense of marginality that the political status of the Niger Delta (as a minority) historically bequeaths to its local (human) subjects. Thus, the persona laments a deep sense of repression, of burden, of being crushed under the weight of limited agency, one that is determined by number. In rectifying this discrepancy between wealth generation and wealth sharing, a rethinking of the geopolitical history of national relation is imperative, for it constitutes the basis upon which the national political process is imagined and performed. Hence, Ikiriko undertakes to reject that history by questioning its foundational politics of exclusion, where the majority takes all at the expense of the minority, conceived as defeated vassals.

Okunoye suggests that "[b]y inserting the idiom of the North/South dichotomy into the context of Nigerian political discourse as a tool for clarifying power relations, Ikiriko finds a binary mode of cognition relevant". Okunoye further insists that "[a]t the heart of this discourse of otherness [in Ikiriko's poetry] is an insinuation of internal colonialism".[247] This offers a fascinating frame for reading this collection; it perhaps explains why the poet tends to personalise the Niger Delta as though it is an extended "self" of the persona. Here, we encounter Ikiriko's preoccupation with minority rights articulated with an aesthetic of geopolitics, one in which the notion of relational complementarity and a sense of belonging in the larger Nigerian project are disavowed and regional otherness is inscribed as the identity marker for the Niger Delta subject. This becomes the subversive strategy by means of which the poet stakes a claim to the oil resource that the region bears, and in which he projects an anti-globalism. Ikiriko takes poetic liberty garnished with a political rhetoric of ethnic, regional consciousness. He creates a narrative of "mythologised victims" in which he stages what Graham Huggan elsewhere describes as a "personal moral crusade against the tyrannies"[248] of global capital on local communities.

In "Oily Rivers", Ikiriko draws on geographic metaphors about the Nigerian map to enact a poetic engagement with this subnational consciousness. He intimates:

> I come from
> the bottom of
> the Amalgam,
> the base Delta,
> where things are made base,
> and beings become base,
> leesed by
> powered policies
> crude as petroleum.[249]

The poem conceives the larger Nigerian geographic entity as literally sitting on the Delta at the "base" of the Nigerian map. This lexical item, "base", is imbued with a subversive aesthetic that is generative and prevailing throughout the poem. This is indicated in the preface to this collection, titled "Foreline",[250] in which Ikiriko gives insight:

> Take a look, dear reader, at the map of Nigeria and behold how the giant country sits, supressing the Delta which serves it the functions of support and sustenance. As it is on the geographical expression, so it is in the political, social and economic expressions.

Thus, by alluding to the Niger Delta as "the bottom of/ the Amalgam",[251] where everyday life is "debased" by facts of geography and geopolitics, Ikiriko finds inspiration in the cartographic logic that expresses the economic condition of the region. In the workings of cartography, the maps (and boundaries) that are produced can, in a counterintuitive way, become nodes for interpreting reality; they allow one to envision that which is not evident, giving concrete expression to what is otherwise elided.[252]

The poet's increasing focus on and obsession with the particularly "debased" state of the Niger Delta, can be gleaned further in the poem "Top Upon Bottom".[253] Here the poet frames the geographical constitution of the South as weakened by the fact of its natural terrain and by virtue of geopolitical status, that is, its inability to influence policies, even ones that directly affect its sociopolitical and economic fortunes. By natural terrain as a fact of the region's weakness is meant that the remoteness of the landscape is a hindrance to development. The Niger Delta consists of mangroves and swamps, with networks of estuaries, labyrinthine creeks and tributaries. This countryside is further afflicted by the "resource curse",[254] in that the enormous wealth generated from oil extraction has not benefitted local livelihood, and in addition, oil effluents blight the environment.

Ikiriko tropes on this weakness using images like "tapering" and "feeble", which are further reinforced by the poet's claim that "we", in the south, have the tendency to be ontologically timid in the sense that "we wobble.../ in associations". Implicit in this poem is the way that the natural location of the Niger Delta impacts on its will to sociality, to act politically; which accounts for its reticence.

If the fact of the Delta's geographical location and natural terrain is responsible for its underdevelopment and provinciality, the poet appears to suggest that the region's relationship to its northerly counterparts is disproportionately uneven. He likens that relationship to one with a giant with unsteady, "feeble feet". His poetry reveals the ways in which two intricate categories of natural and geopolitical concepts, in the form of the natural and the global, combine to define the geopolitical constitution of the Global South in the operation of extraction inspired by globalism. Thus, he signifies the Niger Delta as a place, laying low on the map, constituted to be subservient and antipodal to the Global North, and therefore, diametrically opposite in all things, especially in human development and progress.

But in this act of what I have called a poetics of cartography, there is a disintegration of language in the way Ikiriko deploys word playfulness to make nonsense of the reality that confronts his creative vision. In a sense, the poet is cognisant of the complex nature of his own positioning: that in the ersatz form of globalisation the oil encounter brings into being, the odds are overwhelmingly stacked against local communities whose experiences are elided in its representations. Nevertheless, I read Ikiriko's poetry as a modest contribution to the political, imaginative and ethical attempts to hold extractive capitalism and its free market ethos of open (or in fact, broken) borders into account.

Given the conscious intention to intervene in the political economy of oil extraction in the Niger Delta, Ikiriko's poetry is rendered in the service of that marginalised society and its blighted environment. Deploying multiple voices, it is socially and politically determined. The poetry collection operates on a transgressive impulse to contaminate a daunting experience of the real with counter currents of the "might be" – the "could be" – to make his art carry the burden of his radical intentions. Perhaps this explains John Brannigan's claim in a different context that poetry is "not a passive vehicle of ideological meaning. It generates and multiplies meaning, and therefore must be accounted for as an active participant in the process of fashioning and interpreting society, culture and history".[255] Taken together, *Oily Tears of the Delta* may then be conceived as a poetry of dialogic version and subversion, which springs from, responds to and critiques the form of globalism that constitutes the sites of oil extraction. Indeed, the poetry collection may be read as a cultural artefact primarily produced to subvert the effects of those power-bearing signs that circulate both in the mainstream idiom of geopolitical discourse, and in the local spaces where oil installations are situated.

Conclusion

I have discussed the forms of unseen violence that attend the creative possibilities of Niger Delta poets in their attempts to engage lived experiences in their natal Delta.

I highlighted the ways in which their imagination of local ecology is disrupted by the overwhelming reality of oil extraction, which is framed as a form of unseen violence that underlies the social, political and environmental fault lines enabled and stoked by the corrupting lucre of oil wealth in the Delta. The disruption it brings about in the poetry collections discussed is further observed as one that intrudes on the poets' attempts at laying claim to or establishing a relationship with place. Hence, we notice how in Ojaide's poetry of childhood memory, his relationship with the Delta is intruded upon by the ethical collapse wrought by the changes of oil extraction, and this makes his poem read like a nostalgic evocation. My reading of Ikiriko's poetry shows how the poet challenges the ways in which the logic of this globalised oil infrastructure undermines the daily life of local communities. His narrative stages a dissident act in which ethnic identity is performed to unsettle the notion of placeless-ness as a defining characteristic of the sites in which oil is extracted. His poetry stakes place-specific claims to the environment of the Niger Delta, despite the internationally constituted infrastructure of the oil industry in that locality. This strategy of representing the oil encounter complicates Ghosh's thesis of the oil experience as one that is "lived out within a space that is no place at all…[an] intrinsically displaced" world.[256] Ikiriko's poetry also undermines the logic of the internationally constituted infrastructure of oil production as an enclave unto itself, a formation that Ferguson discusses in *Global Shadows*. Indeed, we see how, unlike most other oil landscapes, the oil infrastructure in the Niger Delta is intimately intertwined with quotidian local existence at the sites of extraction.

What this entails, therefore, is that the sense of intrusion that operates in attempts at registering the impacts of oil extraction in the Delta coerces the poets into incoherence, psychologically alienates and dislocates their memory aid, their mnemonics, from their sense of place – a sense of place invested with local identity and indigenous subjectivity. This, then, represents a profound sense of the "oily" intrusions that operate in the concrete world of the Delta, interrupting, dispossessing and displacing all senses of local existence, including cultural heritage and ecological wellbeing. Indeed, the notion of dispossession is generative, pulling towards what Nixon describes in *Slow Violence and the Environmentalism of the Poor* as "displacement without moving".[257] The notion of displacement thus is a recurring trope in all the poetry collections that capture the oil encounter in the Delta. I now turn to a text that deals with a more spectacular violence as a manifest form of oil intrusion in the Niger Delta.

4 The currency of resistance: Violence as rebellion and commodity

These are revolutionary times. All over the globe men are revolting against old systems of exploitation and oppression and out of the wombs of a frail world new systems of justice and equality are being born. The shirtless and barefoot people of the land are rising up as never before. 'The people who sat in darkness have seen a great light'…We must move past indecision to action…If we do not act, we shall surely be dragged down the long dark and shameful corridors of time reserved for those who possess power without compassion, might without morality, and strength without sight.[258]

This chapter extends conceptions of violence while seeking to understand how it operates in the Niger Delta. It analyses the Nollywood film *The Liquid Black Gold* (2010), focusing on the film's representation of the impacts of petroviolence on local life. Drawing on propositions of violence in the works of Frantz Fanon and Rob Nixon, the chapter situates the film within an intricate climate of dissension and protest, a dichotomy of revolutionary and reprisal violence that attend extractive capitalism's negations in the Delta. Two interlinked interpretations of violence frame the analysis of this film. The first is a well-known and well-documented form of violence in the public sphere. It functions as an agency of civil disobedience deployed by the oppressed, as Fanon tells us in the first chapter of *The Wretched of the Earth,* as an emancipatory mode of apprehending and resisting perceived colonial and imperialist exploitation and oppression. In the Niger Delta, local communities, especially the youth, employ this strategy of resistance violence as a means to transgress state authority and to draw attention to their environments in the throes of ecological destruction. The second sense of violence concerns an exegesis in the context of extraction capitalism and its exactions of local environments such as the Niger Delta. Nixon theorises it as "slow violence", which names and describes, among other issues, environmental pollution, and other degradations in the Global South. According to Nixon, this form of violence, deficient in visibility, complicates conventional acts of confrontation and therefore does not register at all as violence in our knowledge ken, even while possibly more insidious in its impact than physical violence.[259]

The above two senses of violence (Fanon's and Nixon's) pool together in the oil extraction site of the Niger Delta. However, this combination produces a third kind of violence, as will be shown in the analysis of the film text, *The Liquid Black Gold.* As I argue throughout this chapter, this violence stands in-between revolutionary and non-revolutionary violence. It begins as a revolution but later becomes anything but revolutionary. Once it enters the beleaguered space of the oil-impoverished communities, this violence inhabits the agency of the oppressed in their struggle with the forces of power that constellate around oil. Disgruntled and desperate, the restive youth soon produce this violence as a commodity that is circulated and traded alongside the oil commodity. In fact, this violence operates as an entrepreneurial venture of brigandage, generating a cataclysm analogous to the environmental and social impacts of oil extraction in this petroleumscape.

The Liquid Black Gold (producer Ossy Okeke and director Ikenna Aniekwe) centres on a fictional oil-producing community called Zeide. Internal conflicts and other fault lines, including youth unemployment wrought by oil extraction, rive the Zeide community. Embittered, the vibrant members of this community, mostly made up of youth, march to the palace of the community's king to demand a redress of their situation, including accountability in the affairs of local governance. While the king, together with his council of elders, listens to the grievances of the protestors, their leader and the film's protagonist Ebipade (played by Sam Dede) demands a youth representation to the oil company. It is this that catalyses the conflict in the film and results in cataclysmic violence, both internally, among local factions, and externally, with the oil companies and the state.

The protagonist Ebipade presents the discursive construction of the film's positioning of violence in a series of flashbacks and documentary-style narration to his wife, Ihuoma. This provides the justification for the insurgency by the disenchanted, unemployed youth, which includes the destruction of local fishing life and the sexual abuse of women. The film also deals with the corruption and greed of the local chiefs, initially elected to represent the community's interests in their dealings with the oil companies, but now intent on maintaining their *nouveau riche* status. Their corruption is evident at various levels of leadership and power, including in the state army, and in some of the insurgent youth co-opted into these structures.

The plot of *The Liquid Black Gold* reveals the subjectivity of violence in the disputatious politics of oil in postcolonial Nigeria. Government officials, the oil industry operatives, local representatives, and local militias all exploit the fragile conditions under which protests for social and ecological justice take place. This condition of protest becomes in itself the violence, for it is continually unbridled, distracting from the more insidious violence of environmental pollution and economic exploitation in the region.

In the opening sequences of the film, we see the protagonist and dissident youth leader, Ebipade, returning at night from what turns out to be an insurgent mission. He is wearing a balaclava and toting a gun. Upon entering his home, he is confronted by his wife, Ihuoma, with their twelve-year old son, Timipreye, in tow. They are still awake because of the gunshots they are hearing around the neighbourhood. Ihuoma reprimands Ebipade for coming to their home with his "battle gear" on, thereby exposing their son to images of violence. "Must you come back to us wearing that mask, carrying the gun and amulet? You send the wrong message of yourself to our son here", she asks him. "No, I'm sending the right message about myself and my people to him. And that is what I want him to understand, and you too, my wife", Ebipade responds. Presented in this scene is thus a discourse of resistance that articulates from the home space of family life. The film shows how deeply local insurgency is interwoven with domestic life; in the process it offers a moral pertinence to the ecological damage of oil extraction in the Delta. American critique of Nollywood films, Jonathan Haynes says that the domestic space, "narrativized through the marital and family melodrama", has become "the generic bedrock of Nollywood film production".[260] Presented, therefore, in this scene is the domestic space staged as a platform from which local insurgency performs resistance politics. For Ebipade violence is a means of ensuring a future for the young and the unborn, who must grow up to become true beneficiaries of ecological and social justice.

In a dialogue with his family, Ebipade speaks to Timipreye in unequivocal terms about the wisdom of their insurgency:

> *Ebipade*:
>> Hey, come to me my boy. Come here, [*gestures him to sit by his side*] sit down. You haven't said welcome to me.
>
> *Timipreye*:
>> Daddy, welcome.
>
> *Ebipade*:
>> Good. I didn't think you'd still be awake up to this time of the night.
>
> *Timipreye*:
>> I couldn't sleep…the gunshots.
>
> *Ebipade*:
>> The gunshots? But that's the least thing you should worry about, because that is our way of life. It is the only way we can guarantee a better future for our sons. Like you! And for your own sons and the next generation.

Ebipade and his family embody the precariousness of existing in the Niger Delta, demonstrating how local resistance to petro-exploitation destabilises communities' cultural cohesion and unsettles the sanctity of the family unit. The insurgency can sometimes produce hardened militants and brazen criminals in this region. A question is thus raised about Timipreye's future, and his potential inheritance of his father's acts of insurgency, should these issues not be resolved by the time he grows up – if he grows up, that is. Ebipade claims that:

> In some circumstances, yes! Violence can be the only way. We fight to stay alive. We fight to defend ourselves. If anyone dies in the process it only just completes that definition of history: that a few must die for many others to stay alive…In a situation where men are deprived of their land, where women and children are made to drink from polluted swamps just because of oil mining…Yes! – a life can definitely exchange for another life.

Ebipade understands the importance of political power in having one's voice heard. He knows that change and development can only come when someone with the people's interest at heart sits at the discussion table where deliberations with the oil corporations take place. With this in mind, he demands youth representation when the dialogue between the community and the oil corporation will take place. In the presence of the entire community and the council of chiefs, he addresses the king: "The youth of this community have decided that we want to sit and discuss with the Whiteman. Face to face. We do not want any more representatives. And we want to be part of the sharing and distribution process. No more representations". With this demand, Edipade is pitched against the crooked chiefs who represent the community.

The chiefs understand that if they allow the youth to deliberate with the oil companies, their greed and betrayal of the community will be exposed. They connive among themselves to destabilise the brewing resistance and turn the social protest against itself.

> *Chief Zeide:*
> I know that boy will rubbish our effort. That boy has always struck me as a devil. I knew that boy alone would mess up our game.
>
> *Chief Paul (cuts in):*
> But I won't let him; I cannot allow that, that…oh I must do something.
>
> *Chief Ebi:*
> Indeed we must do something. We just have to do something…

So, these chiefs quickly identify a few youths in the community who have benefitted from their corrupt practices. They select these youths to become their stooges and oppose the authentic youth leadership. These youths are mobilised, paid and supplied with guns to cause disunity among the youth group: from here, violence is let loose between the factions. Frustrated by this distracting opposition, Ebipade and his youth followership turn to violence to make their voices heard. Moreover, while the youth continue to believe that the path of dialogue is the best option, the chiefs are bent on destabilising that pursuit for their own benefits. Their decision to employ violence is only vindicated when they are attacked, even while still deliberating on the peaceful means available to them to address the situation. The fighting that ensues distracts them from the real problem they had set out to address in the first place. The youth's frenetic display of energy and indignant exuberance is identified and turned into a commodity as a distractive strategy by the chiefs.

Other interest groups who benefit from the restiveness in the region swoop in to exploit the resistance movement for their parochial benefit. Two other leaders, Ogbuefi and Alhaji, who call themselves "elders representing federal military interests", invite Ebipade to their house and offer to support him only if he decides to take to violence:

> Ogbuefi:
>> So my dear young man, you need to fight, not just to fight but to fight hard. That your so-called chiefs and representatives are ripping you and your entire community off…
>
> Alhaji:
>> You need to fight with all seriousness. We have promised to supply you with guns and ammunition…you need to fight them down and make them respond to the cries of your people.
>
> Ogbuefi:
>> All we need is our commission; [chuckles mischievously] just our commission and we'll give you plenty of ammunition to fight.

As the insurgency degenerates into hostage-taking between the youth factions, the quest to find solutions to the region's environmental and social problems is jettisoned. When Mr Aswani, an expatriate oil company official, shows reluctance to sponsor the insurgency, having been approached by Ebipade to help them get arms and ammunitions, an emissary from his oil-bunkering partners is sent to convince him to let the youths fight. The emissary assures Aswani that, while the government tries to douse the tensions occasioned by the youth insurgency, their oil-bunkering business will go on undetected. What we see here is that, in mediating the spectacle of violence that the youth orchestrate, the film also stages a critique of the latent violence, corruption and exploitation that thrives in this atmosphere of social upheaval. Indeed, embedded within this affective operation of spectacular violence is a powerful politics of bellicosity that both stokes and exploits the conditions within which justice is sought.

Theoretical points of departure

To theorise the practice of violence in the Niger region, I turn to two scholars on the discourses of violence: Fanon and Nixon. Fanon's idea of violence gestures to an emancipatory impulse of defiance against forms of oppression – more precisely, against colonialism and its patrimonies of neoliberal imperialism. Scholars have attempted to antiquate Fanon's idea of violence as an emancipatory mode of apprehending forms of oppression, especially given the rhetoric of terrorism and counterterrorism that underpins contemporary global political discourses.[261] But, as Achille Mbembe has argued,

> It has never been more difficult to read Fanon than it is today, when history seems to be superseded by an infinite present, we need to extricate his work from the ahistorical time frame within which it has been locked in order to make it speak anew.[262]

Mbembe suggests that Fanon might most productively be read in context; one divorced, necessarily, from the (colonial) times in which he wrote and properly situated in the temporal setting to which we want to engage his work. Following Mbembe, my reading of Fanon is situated in the context of the contemporary historical moment in the Niger Delta – in the context of petro-induced violence, which simultaneously elicits both revolutionary and reactionary violence at the site of petropolitics, the one becoming epiphenomenal of the other.

Fanon's theory of resistance violence can be read fruitfully in the present-day context of the Niger Delta, enabling an understanding of the debates inaugurated by the twin issues of environmental and social injustice occasioned by oil extraction and the geopolitics that enable its operations. These issues feature as a new form of colonialism; thus, the interventions deployed to resist oil extraction evoke an anticolonial temperament. The resistance struggles against petro-exploitation currently emanating from the Niger Delta find resonance, in other words, with a Fanonian vocabulary of anti-colonialism. As such, the present agitation for justice in the Delta is "a liberation struggle of a special type: liberation from internal colonialism, poverty, wretchedness and an empty future".[263]

For Fanon, violence is the structural manifestation of forms of oppression and domination of peoples, cultures and nations by colonialism. Fanon notes that these oppressions, once conceived as violence, cannot be defeated outside the purview of revolutionary violence, which acts as a progressive vehicle through which freedom is attained and the humanity of the oppressed is re-instated. Humanity, after all, has the proclivity for freedom. Where freedom is denied, people feel constricted, a limitation that diminishes their being. Attempting to re-humanise the self, the oppressed tend to resort to that which bespeaks their state of subjection: violence. This kind of violence, Fanon argues, becomes the means by which they repossess their humanity. Fanon does not see this violence as an end; he insists that it secures the possibility for structural and practical transformation, which operate outside of a politics of negation, oppression and exploitation. These forms of violence serve as incongruous modes of distraction, both to the resistance groups and their perceived villains. The insurgency, which members of the local community deploy to disavow this politics of negation and make visible the deep structural violence, is one consumed by the spectacle of that visibility. Civil disobedience insulates the main issues of social and environmental injustice from public scrutiny and usurps the rebellion deployed to bring it about.

In *Liquid Black*, the youth's eventual resort to violence echoes Jean-Paul Sartre's dictum in his preface to Fanon's *Wretched of the Earth* that "no gentleness can efface the marks of violence [slow violence]; only violence [sabotage] itself can destroy them [marks of violence]".[264] Sartre notes that irrepressible violence is not man's degeneracy to savagery, nor a misguided resentment of constituted authority; it is his resolve to re-create himself in the face of oppression.[265] Drawing on this idea, *Liquid Black* frames the operation of violence not as an instrument of decolonisation in a strict Fanonian sense, but as a form of resisting ecological devastation and resource colonialism evident in the petro-industrial complex in Nigeria.

If, in the Fanonian paradigm, social protest and subversion are the uses to which violence is put in the film, violence also features as an analogous phenomenon to the oil commodity. This form of violence is woven around the visible damage done to the environment as well as the socio-cultural upheavals wrought on the human inhabitants. Nixon frames this as "slow violence", which has consequently elicited an environmentalism of the poor in the spaces where it is perceived and made manifest. The introductory chapter of this book discusses the form of environmental consciousness projected in literary and cultural expressions of the Niger Delta. It depicts the social and environmental fault lines of oil extraction. Drawing on Nixon's *Slow Violence and the Environmentalism of the Poor,* I posited how these fault lines in the Delta articulate as a kind of violence more insidious in its impact on quotidian life and the local environment. Nixon's analysis brings into productive dialogue conceptions of nature and the social contexts within which the environment is imagined.

This idea is significant to my analysis of *Liquid Black,* for it is environmental pollution and the destruction of the agrarian and fishing economy that exacerbate existing agitations, which progress into physical violence in the film. Nixon's coinage of "slow violence" complicates conventional assumptions about violence as a highly visible act of confrontation. His theory offers alternative insights into theorising environmental pollution as a form of violence, enabling us to locate the modes of counter-discursive narratives that operate in the film's allegorising protocol of violence. The concept of slow violence allows us to rethink social afflictions as violence, even when these do not otherwise register within the ken of what counts as violence. Inequitable resource distribution is a form of violence that is non-physical and deficient in visibility, but nonetheless atrocious in its effect – impoverishing and dehumanising those without voice or other instruments of peaceful resistance.[266]

Liquid Black frames violence as something elicited by various factors issuing from the operations and politics of oil production in the Niger Delta. The video film reveals how the primary grievances of the Zeide community revolve around issues of environmental pollution and social disruption, which are occasioned by oil extraction. These problems are deemed to operate as a complex structurally orchestrated malaise that Nixon frames as "slow violence", an "environmentally embedded violence that is often difficult to source, oppose…and reverse".[267] The film highlights how attempts at making these valences of slow violence visible through the instrumentality of popular revolt and dissidence meet with physical violence, with both acts of resistance having a cataclysmic effect on the Zeide community and its environment. In this sense, the film can be viewed as offering a modest answer to Nixon's call for representational intervention in instances of slow violence. As Nixon suggests, artists – both literary and visual – need be actively creative in drawing public attention to catastrophic acts that are low in instant spectacle but high in long-term effects.

Liquid Black is unable, however, to draw public attention to the slow violence of environmental degradation, as the film's action is quickly overtaken by physical violence and insurgency amongst the youth factions. The film shows violence as an entrepreneurial enterprise by which unemployed and disgruntled youth find release, one that soon degenerates into brazen criminality and brigandage. Violence is shown in the film to be encouraged and stoked by a dynamic of power tussle amongst the local leaders, which does nothing to address the initial problems of ecological wellbeing and unemployment in the community. The community leaders fight about who must represent the community and what points of interests and demands must be presented before the oil companies. Subsequently, the personal interests of the select representative appear to prevail over the interests of collective. In this way, the film succeeds in drawing attention to the increasing uselessness of cultural structures meant to uphold order in the face of changing dynamics motivated by self-interest on the parts of local chiefs and military leaders.

The film portrays the community king as useless and ignorant, and easily swayed by his crooked advisers, a troika of chiefs, namely Chief Zeide, Chief Paul and Chief Ebi. The king is isolated in his palace and relies on the lies these chiefs feed him, signalling the ascendancy of political and economic power over cultural power in African modernity. Monarchs, supposedly the custodians of cultural values and societal cohesion, are rendered powerless, if not altogether useless, in the socio-political economy of modern oil states, such as postcolonial Nigeria, whose fundamental cultural and traditional foundations are being hollowed out by the muck of oil politics.

Nollywood and the politics of mediation

My intention in this section is not to foray into the evolution of Nollywood as a cultural knowledge site and formidable medium of representation in Nigeria. That subject is addressed adequately in previous studies.[268] Rather, I wish to examine an aspect of its production that draws on the aesthetics of the melodramatic to attend to instances of protest for environmental and social justice in Nigeria. My interest resides in the modalities through which violence signifies in *Liquid Black* as a countercultural "discursive construction that creates and institutionalises this episteme [of violence] as discourse".[269] The film brings into relief how violence, both epistemologically and materially, can be read as a pervasive agency in the politics of representation, axiomatically rampant and libidinous. This category of violence has become the currency circulating in exchange for control over the oil wealth. Perhaps as a way to remedy this operation of violence, *Liquid Black* has harnessed its massive Nollywood viewing audience to represent the counter-cultural narration that articulates local resistance politics, acting as a filmic platform through which the realities of oil extraction are re-enacted for public scrutiny. As Chukwuma Okoye shows, "video film production is one such vigorous informal means by which ordinary people productively contest their precarious social and cultural conditions".[270]

If there is any local integrity and indigenous power that might be associated with Nollywood films, then *Liquid Black* appears strategically produced as a means of isolating the social malaise of violence exacerbated by crude extraction for a targeted audience's scrutiny. To be sure, there is a particular geopolitical interest in the Niger Delta struggles, and, if successfully realised, it attunes to the concerns of local communities. Nollywood thus seems to be a powerful vehicle through which to engage and apprehend the social and political fault lines of oil extraction. In a sense, *Liquid Black* presents an influential, if nuanced dimension, in representing instances of violence that attend to the oil encounter in Nigeria. It is, therefore, not by mere coincidence that most of the films that deal with themes of petroviolence and debates around resource control are written, produced, and directed by mostly the same individuals and acted by mostly the same cast.[271]

There is a necessary organisation of productive forces in the film industry of Nollywood; this reflects the imbalances in the Nigerian national polity. Actors, directors, scriptwriters, and producers who are from minority groups are subsumed under a national cinema culture and unable to project their cultural specificities. This is a powerful sentiment among Nollywood practitioners who are from minority groups, and I suggest that *Liquid Black* represents a response to that phenomenon. Most Nollywood productions are sponsored by indigenous producers "who practically dictate the type of plot they want to see in the production".[272] Nollywood's global circulation is thus mobilised to benefit the local in this film, serving a bridge between what is simultaneously site-specific and has international traction. According to Okome, Nollywood generates:

> knowledge at the local about the global that has eluded the watchful eyes
> of the state and corporate capital. Nollywood surely produces its own
> brand of knowledge in the competitive environment of the production
> of visual knowledge. It generates its own sense of the logic of the human
> condition in a postcolonial situation.[273]

Liquid Black, in a similar way, refracts the concept of violence in a manner that subverts and destabilises the discursive idiom of youth insurgency in the Niger Delta. Here, the meta-narrative of violence around which the politics of oil extraction is inscribed in the Delta is wrestled from the public domain and re-appropriated to address the concerns of the local. Within this this postcolonial condition of social disorder and political restiveness, violence is invested with a new grammar that not only negotiates the heroic struggle for the remediation of the polluted environment and local control of oil, but also brings into relief the paradoxes of local militarisation and brigandage that exacerbate the conditions it purports to challenge.

Dialogue, storytelling and the mediation of violence in Liquid Black

In what appears to be a technological deficiency in giving filmic realisation to instances of violence, *The Liquid Black Gold* deploys narrative characteristics of dialogue, storytelling and narrative embedding to stage and contextualise the manner of its operations in the struggle for justice. What the film lacks in cinematic techniques, such as giving visual images to the oil pollutions of the Delta rivers, the gas flaring into the atmosphere, or even the violent confrontations between insurgent factions, it makes up for in dialogue. The film imbues Ebipade with the art of telling – of narrating, not necessarily showing, except by facial and hand gestures – as would a griot in an oral performance. This speaks to Nollywood's speed and immediacy in responding to, and drawing materials from, topical matters in Nigeria.

Ebipade is made the speaking subject through whom the film's discursive intentions are projected in a way that suggests the immediacy of a direct, live, dialogue with the audience – although this takes place in a conversation with his wife Ihuoma. In one scene, Ebipade has just returned from an insurgent expedition and his wife is uncomfortable with the spiral of violence in which the resistance is embroiled. She reprimands him for turning against his own people, whom Ebipade deems as traitors who have colluded with the government and oil multinationals to exploit their community. Ihuoma charges Ebipade,

> You so stoutly justify and defend the actions of you and
> your boys, Ebipade? Even when you fight and kill your own
> brothers and sisters? People who you should be with in this
> so-called struggle?

Ebipade:
> Yes, because those brothers and sisters who should be with us in
> this noble struggle have turned around to kick our backs.

The Liquid Black Gold presents Ihuoma as a voice of alternative advocacy. This depiction is obviously gendered and possibly problematic; but her participation is, nonetheless, instrumental in the struggle, for she is the one who repeatedly offers Ebipade the medium to rationalise their insurgency. Agatha Ukata interrogates the portrayal of women in Nollywood films, noting that such representations derive from, and reinforce, stereotypical notions about women's subservience to men in patriarchal African societies.[274] Such stereotypical gender dichotomies are also at play in this film, for Ihuoma signifies as the listening subject to Ebipade. However, in my view Ihuoma is playing an equally important role in the film. Given the artistic limitations of Nollywood films, Ihuoma's character becomes inventive in stimulating Ebipade to enter into monologue, through subjective focalisation, in which the actions of the film are recounted. Ebipade is positioned here, following Bakhtin, as the "speaking subject whose utterance"[275] provides the necessary rationale for violence, an aspect which Liquid Black is unable to give filmic realisation to. Thus, he becomes the medium through whom the deficiency in the film's ability to visually represent (slow) violence is mitigated. Ebipade's dialogue in the film is interspersed with camera movement, which pans out in a montage sequence to give motion descriptions of his verbal accounts.

The motion images, used in segues from Ebipade's verbal accounts to Ihuoma about the instances of the violence that he describes, are at best amateurish. The film takes seem like real-life events, captured without rehearsals or multiple shots. Although the mutual intersection of Ebipade's telling and the camera intervention in refracting tropes of violence in the film may seem technically weak, the film is able to realise its artistic intentions. In a sense, it indicates that the breaks in Ebipade's verbal accounts, caused by the camera montage, do not suggest that he lacks the discursive grammar to articulate the ideology of their resistance, but that Nollywood production, while taking cognisance of its technological limitations in representing violence, deploys modes of oral rendition to complement its visual portrayal. Thus, the film's medium of portraying violence is what I have chosen to describe as "oraltronics": a representational protocol that blends oral rendition with electronic mediation of video film. Both are deployed "to perform the work the film needs to do and to reflect on",[276] namely the mutual intersection between Nollywood production and its preceding tradition of African oral forms. What we see here is that this griotic function is not visibly apparent in the film; rather it is implied in a manner that is nuanced and subtle.

Crucially, there is a narrative structure embedded in the film and most of the action is woven around it. This narrative structure is, in turn, organised around Ebipade's account to Ihuoma. Although Ebipade is the one who speaks, he is always responding to what has been said before, both by his wife and by all the critiques made of insurgent violence; in that sense, his rendition is highly dialogic. At this stage, the film does not seem to be concerned much with what it projects or what it is saying, but with *how* it is said. Ebipade faces the camera and addresses his assumed audience as if he were on a live stage. Here, the film seems to break with filmic conventions of the fictive, the make-believe, seen through the eye of the camera. Its break with the filmic mode of the fictive would seem that its aim is to pass a message in a manner that conveys the political urgency of the real. Where the film is unable to show spectacles of violence or give filmic realisation to slow violence, Ebipade's commentary interjects to give creative expression to that which the film attempts to refract.

Storytelling is an art in representing lived experience and may be used to understand how the tropes of violence – which elude graphic mediation – are captured in the film. In his reflection on the fictional works of the nineteenth-century Russian novelist Nicolai Leskov, Walter Benjamin discusses the writer's artistry in capturing the integrity and essence of experience through an uncommon craftsmanship in telling stories.[277] Benjamin notes that "The storyteller takes what he tells from experience – his own or that reported by others. And he in turn makes it the experience of those who are listening to his talk".[278] When he draws a distinction between the storyteller and the one who merely informs, Benjamin excellently captures how central the art of storytelling is in representing the lived experiences of the oil encounter narratives in the Niger Delta, which sometimes elude mediation:

> It is half the art of storytelling to keep a story free from explanation
> as one reproduces it…The most extraordinary things, marvellous
> things, are related with the greatest accuracy, but the psychological

> connection of the events is not forced on the reader. It is left up to him
> to interpret things the way he understands them, and thus the narrative
> achieves an amplitude that information lacks...The value of information
> does not survive the moment in which it was new. It lives only at that
> moment; it has to surrender to it completely and explain itself to it
> without losing any time. A story is different. It does not expend itself.
> It preserves and concentrates its strength and is capable of releasing it
> even after a long time.[279]

Confronted with the technological challenge of making a graphic statement in the
film about the environmental and the social injustice experienced in Zeide, the
Nollywood film imbues Ebipade with uncommon craftsmanship in chronicling the
oil encounter in Zeide. In this sense, the film reminds viewers that "story-telling is
always the art of repeating stories, and this art is lost when the stories are no longer
retained. It is lost because there is no more weaving and spinning to go on while they
are being listened to".[280] The inability of Nollywood to graphically capture the slow
violence in the Delta is compensated for, in other words, by Ebipade's craftsmanship
in relating the narrative to viewers. He makes his role in the struggle marginal,
while maintaining the importance of the agitation to the realisation of justice for the
environmental and social destructions that have taken place in the Delta.

Following Benjamin, the meaning of Ebipade's life and his experience with the oil
encounter (that is, the agitations and the brazen violence) is revealed only in the
struggle he throws his life into. According to Benjamin, a storyteller does not tell the
audience what they do not already know, but does it with such skill that

> The storytelling that thrives for a long time in the circle of work –
> the rural, the maritime, and the urban – is itself an artisan form of
> communication, as it were. It does not aim to convey the pure essence of
> the thing, like information or a report. It sinks the thing into the life of
> the storyteller, in order to bring it out of him again. Thus the traces of the
> storyteller cling to the story the way the handprints of the potter cling to
> the clay vessel. Storytellers tend to begin their story with a presentation
> of the circumstances in which they themselves have learned what is to
> follow, unless they simply pass it off as their own experience.[281]

The above lines illuminate how Ebipade narrates the story of Zeide community
within the context of the upheavals that the oil encounter exacerbates. The struggle
for justice in the Delta becomes a struggle for his own life; he does not tell us what
we do not already know. Ebipade weaves and spins the story through his own
involvement in the resistance, so that the Niger Delta struggle becomes a fresh tale
of the oil encounter. Through his storytelling, one is able to establish how violence
is deployed, paradoxically, as a commodity as well as a rebellious instrument in
the hands of the agitating youth and the oppressive order they set out to resist in
the first instance.

Through this technique of narration, the oil encounter is re-enacted experientially in what unfolds in the film, to lay bare the banality of violence. Benjamin says, "All great storytellers have in common the freedom with which they move up and down the rungs of their experience as on a ladder".[282] He argues further that a great storyteller embodies "the image for a collective experience to which even the deepest shock of every individual experience, death, constitutes no impediment or barrier"[283] in producing sets of cognitive meaning for understanding complex encounters such as those evoked by the oil phenomenon in the Niger Delta.

Transgression as a subversive strategy against regimes of power has never been a static phenomenon; it is in constant flux. Therefore, the dissidents involved have multiple subjectivities, which are sometimes conflicting. The characters embody the paradoxes that attend the ontology of oil in the Delta – heroism and villainy, integrity and compromise, wealth and poverty, morality and amorality, husbands and insurgents – all at the same time. Hence, Tejumola Olaniyan argues in another context that, "Even so, whether ankle-or neck-deep in complicity, there is always a complicity, for the ground of resistance is veritably impure".[284]

This ground of complicity is cogent in understanding the seemingly contradictory roles Ebipade plays in the film, for he embodies the contradictions and inconsistencies inherent in the oil encounter. Much as Ebipade is the leader of the dissident youth and the "supreme commander" of the foot soldiers in the Delta creeks, his humanity and moral standing are in no way brought into question. That his wife reprimands him at home suggests that he considers her as an equal partner in the domestic sphere, precisely because it seems important to him that she understands the driving force behind his insurgency. Therefore, he does not impose himself and his beliefs on her; but he makes it a point of duty to explain the complexity of violence in the community. Moreover, this, in a sense, illustrates the dichotomy of husband and insurgent in Ebipade's character.

Although Ebipade is ideologically motivated and morally upright, he is by no means perfect. He is not a flat character. We see how he develops as the plot unravels, so that the moral hero that emerges at the end of the film is one who has been shaped by the unfolding actions: local political tension, violent confrontations between factions and eventual resolution. He is perceptive, for he understands the enormity of the task he is faced with. As such, he demands youth representation and the seeking of social justice throughout the insurgency. For instance, Ebipade's decision to avenge the betrayal and murder of his friend and "sergeant-at-arms", Layefah, pushes him to re-strategise. He compromises as a means of sustaining the resistance only when such a move ensures his continuous formidability against his assailants, and this means that he is able to hold a firm stance to its conclusive end.

When, as the film refers, the "elders who represent powerful interest from above," decide to stop financing their struggle, he plays an ace card from his hand that will ensure the continuous flow of arms and ammunition for the cause. Firstly, he seeks a youth representation among the community delegation to the oil company to deliberate and negotiate without violence, as a peaceful means of remedying the effects of oil extraction on the community. When the chiefs scuttle this approach, he agrees to be supplied with ammunition by the two elders, Alhaji and Ogbuefi, as a desperate move to make the youth's voices heard and bring attention to their concerns.

He strikes a deal with Mr Aswani, an official of the oil multinational believed to be in connivance with some local elites to bunker oil in the region. Ebipade agrees to turn a blind eye in return for arms and ammunition to sustain the rebellion. At this stage, the film creates a context for insurgency in the region and serves as a subtext to the dubious role which violence plays in perpetuating an atmosphere of restiveness that makes meaningful development in the region impossible. However, even as the youth resistance turns to brigandage, Ebipade's actions do not degenerate into acts of greed or parochial interests; they become acts of strategic sabotage as a means of pushing forward his community's demands.

Even while he is detained without trial – after being deceived out of the creeks by the cunning chiefs – his followers remain loyal to him. They frame Ebipade's unlawful detention as a strategic game of war. They, too, deploy their own tactics of kidnapping and hostage-taking, by kidnapping expatriate officials of the oil multinationals, who hitherto have been left out of the insurgency. The youths see the violent confrontations between factions and the dubious chiefs as a sort of witty game; thus, they deploy metaphors of sport contest to articulate their resistance.

When the second-in-command, Biokpor, is approached to cease hostility by Chief Teride, the new government-appointed negotiator, Biokpor tells of his readiness to "play the game [of war] when the whistle is blown", that there is "no game [of peace] unless Ebipade is released". This suggests that, since Ebipade is the initiator of the insurgency demanding environmental and social justice, he is also seen as pivotal to the resolution of conflict and a key figure in the entrenchment of true justice and meaningful development in his community. Thus, his involvement in the story – and his account of it – becomes a mirror through which the complex tale of the operations of petroviolence in the Delta might be understood.

Embedded narrative of internal violence as critique of nationalist ideologies

In *Liquid Black* the logic of local integrity and indigenous power of Nollywood films are reinforced through the film's utilisation of first-rate actors, who are eminent as members of its cast. There seems to be a predetermined credibility to the oppositional discursive tropes of violence that the film engages. The personalities behind the characters in the film have a cameo-like characteristic, although they play major roles in the film. They command some respect, if not reverence, in the Niger Delta and even in mainstream Nigerian society. By way of illustration Sam Dede, one of the foremost actors in Nollywood, plays Ebipade. Dede is also a professor of drama at the University of Port Harcourt, a major tertiary institution located in the oil capital of Nigeria, Port Harcourt. Justus Esiri, one of the pioneering actors in Nollywood, plays Chief Ebi. Esiri was a veteran theatre and film actor who died in 2012. These personalities have some force of authority – and they give weight to the characters they play in the film. Provided with a medium to express the disaffection of the Delta to Ihuoma, Ebipade constructs an argument framed in the politics of minority resistance:

Ebipade:
> Let me tell you something my dear wife, our real enemies are the government and those that we have sent to represent us before the oil companies. Our perceived enemies are the oil companies, who out of naivety or ignorance, or, maybe, sheer greed, have connived with these two enemies to rip us off. There was a clause in the 1963 Constitution and that clause gave us the power to control the resources in our region. That power was also vested in other regions. You see, when agriculture was the mainstay of our country's economy, nobody, nobody amended or abrogated that section of the constitution. But at the advent of oil in the Zeide Region...let's not even go into that...Let me tell you something, resource control is the remote and immediate solution to all this crisis.

Ebipade's address to his wife finds exteriority in the vexed discourse about resource control, but he is unable to follow it through. The film seems to wrestle his account from the concrete materiality of the region's geopolitical history of tensions with the Nigerian state over revenue sharing. Nevertheless, it soon morphs into a mystifying discourse of resistance that is contradictory in its articulation.[285] The context of the film's material production and the discursive conditions it summons gesture to an atmosphere of the paradoxical and the unresolvable exacerbated by the oil encounter in Nigeria.

For instance, within the context of violent resistance that the film refracts, there is an embedded narrative of that internally stoked violence that it portrays and critiques. Throughout the film there tends be a departure from the familiar script of blaming the oil multinationals as the identifiable culprit in the environmental pollution and destruction of the social fabric in the Delta. *Liquid Black* thus constructs an oppositional discourse of violence instigated by internal tensions between the youth and their local elders in the communities.

Furthermore, *The Liquid Black Gold* also gives an imaginative realisation to an important, but often ignored, aspect of the Niger Delta crisis: a generational ideological rivalry between young and old. This rivalry stems from a culture of gerontocracy in African societies but is increasingly being displaced, through post-traditional African modernity. It has fuelled many of the internal tensions that result in brigandage among youth groups in the Delta. Here, again, Ihuoma provides the podium for Ebipade to articulate this ironic twist in the insurgency. Without her prompting, Ebipade's eventual actions would not make sense to the audience. "Tell me about your brothers and sisters who you kill and kidnap," she urges her husband.

> Ebipade:
>> They are just a lucky few who the community appointed to bring
>> before the oil company the several hardships oil exploration
>> has brought on our people: Chief Ebi, Chief Zeide and Paul,
>> a retired schoolteacher. They have become so rich; they are
>> even richer than the king. And they saw this assignment as an
>> opportunity to enrich themselves while shutting their ears to the
>> plights of our people.

This passes a damning commentary on the avarice of local community representatives and government officials sent to intervene in intra-community crises in parts of Nigeria. In the same vein, Ebipade's submission here complicates the endless story of greed, corruption and betrayal that accompany Nigeria's oil encounter.

The film crystallises, then, into a critique of Nigeria's nationalism; it brings to the fore the weakness in the argument of local claim over oil against national interest. The local claim to oil wealth is set up against national interest, which is a problematic notion. The embedded narrative of this internally stoked violence portrays a profound crisis of ethical life in the Niger Delta, which has continued to be insulated from critical scrutiny by the more media-friendly issue of environmental pollution. Since the local community cannot produce responsible representative leadership who can genuinely champion the cause of the Niger Delta, *Liquid Black* suggests that the utopian event of an actual total control of the oil resource by the Niger Delta would be counterproductive. Some of the local leaders would expropriate the wealth for their selfish benefits. And this would, no doubt, result in a more disturbing spectacle of fratricide and patricide.

Traditional structure of hierarchy in African modernity is being put on trial in this film. There is a powerful tension between gerontocratic rule in African societies and modern postcolonial conditions where the youth, increasingly disillusioned because they cannot find jobs, believe that the elders grab power for themselves and are indifferent to their plights. The youth feel that traditional societies have continued to deploy cultural politics and contrived traditional customs to disenfranchise them in local governance. The ascendancy of community elders over youths, who have more vitality and are often better skilled, with superior education and exposure, has been a major source of conflict in the Niger Delta.[286] *Liquid Black* portrays this generational tension.

Due to the long years of neglect and the mistrust that oil extraction has engendered, the problems of the Niger Delta have transcended those of structural development. It has come to the level where the so-called resource rebels have begun to see their insurgency as a career, a means of livelihood. When a structural solution is proffered without taking into consideration the social, economic and moral burden such old agitations have brought to this troubled society, this becomes a problematic situation.

In *Liquid Black*, the rebelling factions succeed in enacting an insidious form of violence that Fanon may not have envisaged. Fanon frames the use of violence as a strategy that might lead to freedom and an entrenchment of political consciousness, based on equal participation of all revolutionaries, that is, of all citizens. However, violence in the film has become political in and of itself, enabling the feuding parties to partake in the revenue sharing (or grabbing) of oil proceeds, and thereby reduces the value of the ideals around which Fanon's notions of decolonisation are framed. In this sense, the film enacts Fanon's anticipation, in the third chapter of *Wretched of the Earth*, where he warns against a chauvinistic nationalism that is devoid of social and political consciousness, but one that is cynically bourgeois, lazy and opportunistic.[287] Take, as an example, the characters of Eriye and Akpobome, the leaders of the hirelings fighting on the side of the chiefs, who see their newly acquired power as a form of economic opportunity. They consider violence as a source of income because, in the event of a favourable consideration of their demands, they might not be able to get a job in the oil companies: they lack the requisite qualifications to become paid employees. Both men thus consider Ebipade an economic rival who is bent on sabotaging their means of survival. What begins as a rebellion against injustice, therefore becomes rivalry between factions, a personal fight for unhindered access to, and control of, the perks that revolutionary opportunism (in this case, as thugs to the oil nouveau riche) brings.

Natural resources and oil wars

There is the involvement of a global cartel of oil bunkering that fuels and finances militancy, thereby making illicit trade in crude oil possible because of the porous security situation occasioned by youth upheavals.[288] With detailed analyses of facts, figures and concrete examples, Abiodun Alao discusses the relationship between natural resources and conflicts in Africa, of which Nigeria, with its vast oil reserve, is a case in point. He identifies three weaknesses in governance concerning natural resources that fuel violent confrontations in Nigeria: the inadequacy of laws and regulations governing the sharing of the endowment, the intricacies of elite politics and the changing role of civil society.[289] Alao concedes that the problems he has identified are part of the complicated conflicts. He goes on to proffer possible solutions to ending these conflicts, namely the establishment of "credible structures" that can assist in ensuring equal distribution of Nigeria's resources. However, Alao is oblique in proposing a concrete approach to addressing the crisis of insurgency. Establishing credible structures to address the crisis in Niger Delta has not yielded any lasting solutions: several interventionist commissions have been established in the last few decades to address questions of social development and revenue distribution in the oil producing regions of the Delta.[290] However, they have turned out to be mere political propaganda whose programmes have not gone beyond the jingles by which they are announced in the media. Often, their perfunctory efforts have been easily thwarted because they have lacked the moral will to do good or even to gain genuine understanding of the region's challenges.

The social and ecological crisis in Niger Delta consist of a web of fluid dynamics "in which global forces are implicated in, and benefit from, oil extracted under conditions of structural violence and iniquity".[291] Oil bunkering, an illicit trade in crude oil, is made possible through security lapses occasioned by local resistance and insurgency and has become a major financier of militancy in this region. The smuggling cartel is believed to include officials of the Nigerian state and some big players in transnational oil circuits, both within the country and in far-flung oil futures markets in London, Detroit, Rotterdam and Brazil. These business-oriented individuals benefit from the restiveness and lax security situation in the Niger Delta. Even when the Nigerian state is sincere about addressing the myriads problems oil extraction causes, it is soon distracted from the illicit trade by its showdown with the resource rebels and insurgent groups in the region.

In the Delta, groups of criminal elements within the ranks of the youth, who are mostly ex-political thugs, have had an enormously negative impact on the conflict over resource control.[292] These criminals have capitalised on the restive situation of an otherwise instructive insurgency and employed criminal tactics, including the kidnapping of innocent, well-meaning individuals – foreigners and locals. This has brought disrepute to the rebels and greatly compromised their supposedly noble struggles. In his role as executive director of Environmental Rights Action, Nnimmo Bassey says,

> The current violent confrontations in the Niger Delta appear to have taken on a life that the instigators could not have predicted and the smoke of battle is so thick and the tricky creeks so murky that pinpointing combatants on either side is a difficult business.[293]

The messy business of monumentalising the combatants as untainted heroes in the resistance struggles bears out in *Liquid Black*. We notice how the youth leader, Biokpor, and his fellow combatants, fighting on the side of Ebipade, easily relapse into the killing and kidnapping of their opponents, as soon as Ebipade is arrested and kept in military custody. This compromises the integrity of their initial demands; little room is left for the course of justice to ultimately prevail, which is what they seek in the first instance.

In a sense, this is where the third category of violence begins to take form in the film. It is neither revolutionary nor non-revolutionary; rather it stands in between. This third form of violence begins as a revolution but later becomes anything but revolutionary. It is not completely hijacked by criminal elements among the youth movement, nor is it entirely overtaken by parochial interests. Violence in this atmosphere of rage soon degenerates to sheer brigandage, pulling towards the murk of all that it seeks to challenge in the first instance. That is where such violence becomes a parallel commodity traded amongst the feuding parties, exploiting the rebellion deployed to bring it about.

In *Liquid Black,* Ebipade and his youth movement resort to violence when their quest for deliberative democracy and justice for their community is scuttled by the chiefs who represent them. Yet without their knowing it, their choice of resistance violence is exploited by those who benefit from the lopsided socio-political economy of the Niger Delta. The chiefs, having enriched themselves at the expense of the community, raise a counter-force from among the agitating youth group to cause disunity in their midst and distract them from their quest. When the chiefs and the youth have an audience with the king, the chiefs plant a seed of doubt as to who should lead the youth delegation. The film depicts the subtlety of the chiefs' plans, because no one in the youth group realises that they are being pitted against each other. Again, the need for and access to power (economic and political) is depicted as a strong motivation. Ogbuefi and Alhaji who, according to the film, "represent interests from above" offer to equip the youths with arms to continue the mortal combat, thereby buying into this commodity of violence as a means of distracting from the main issues of slow violence, which the uprising was meant to address. Thus, the youth are completely distracted from addressing the subtle violence that produced the conditions for social disorder and the collapse of ethical life in their community.

Local resistance, politics of neoliberalism and global circuit of extraction

The Liquid Black Gold depicts in a generative way the incongruous nature of violence, including its physical, social and environmental forms. Violence has tended to be the very condition under which the globally constituted business of oil production is conducted in the Delta region. There are local and global forces "enmeshed and implicated in the [oil-related] violent conflict either as supporters of the state-backed transnational extractors of oil or as allies of local resistance movements and rights advocacy groups",[294] who exploit the fragile security situation in the region to serve their selfish ends. In what he calls "extractive neoliberalism", James Ferguson reflects on the untidy atmosphere produced by oil related conflicts that enables "flexible and opportunistic forms of deregulated enterprises to flourish in Africa".[295] He notes that the peculiar nature of oil extraction, and the manner in which it is insulated from the local realities in the parts of Africa where it is produced, has facilitated new forms of spatial flexibility made possible by neoliberal conventions of deregulated markets and the free movement of capital across "broken borders".[296]

It is instructive to note that even when the local crises are fuelled by oil extraction, the industry is intractably insulated from the crisis its operations stoke and exacerbate. This point finds resonance in a real-life incident cited in Timothy Hunt's *Politics of Bones*, a biography of Owens Wiwa, the younger brother of Ken Saro-Wiwa. The book is a protest testimony of the role played by the younger Wiwa in the Ogoni struggle with the Nigerian state in the 1990s. Hunt narrates an altercation between a group of Ogoni farmers and a group of Wilbros Construction expatriate workers and their military guards. Owens intervenes after some protesting locals were shot at by the company's security:

> As they spoke, Owens noticed a group of women crying over another woman who was lying on the ground. Trying not to show his anger, Owens asked the army captain if it would be all right if he spoke with the man in charge of the Wilbros workers. "That's the manager there," said the captain, pointing to one of the white men in a shirt and tie. Owens introduced himself. "Tell me what's happening. I had some people who came to my clinic who said they were shot. Now I come here and I'm seeing this. What is it? The man, whose name was J.K. Tillery, shrugged and said, "Hey, this is none of my business." "How do you mean?" "These are Nigerian soldiers and these are Nigerian people. It's none of my business." "Sir, I passed this road yesterday and your trucks were not here," said Owens. "These soldiers were not here and these people were not here. Nobody was shot. You brought the soldiers to this area. So now, this is your business."[297]

Drawing a parallel with *Liquid Black*, it becomes apparent that the oil multinationals – referenced in the metaphor of "The Whiteman" – are not drawn directly into the conflict in the film. Instead, *The Liquid Black Gold* focuses on the internal crisis of local greed as a veritable, if more insidious, violence; a cultural crisis in oil-bearing communities generating just as more discontents as the pollution of their environment by oil effluents. Moreover, it is only when "The Whiteman" is taken hostage by the agitating youth, as a desperate move to force the government to address their concerns, that the conflict is resolved, and the film comes to an end. The kidnapped official is instrumental in ending the conflict. He is the one who finally manages to get a peace-brokering deal underway, which leads to the release of Ebipade and the award of contracts for structural developments in the Zeide community. In this sense, *Liquid Black* appears to avoid an overt critique of neoliberal capitalism and its regime of oil governance in the Delta. Nevertheless, the film is nuanced in its portrayal of Big Oil as amoral in its approach to business in the Delta.

Fanon observes how neoliberalism, with its vestiges of colonial imperium, always succeeds in safeguarding "their legitimate interests [in former colonies] with the help of [certain] economic conventions",[298] albeit Western-invented conventions. Hence, there appears to be reluctance verging on indifference on the part of the multinationals in intervening in the conflicts between the Nigerian state and the local communities. The oil corporations always pride themselves on being anything but meddlesome; they argue that they are there to do business and make profit, and not to meddle into issues of social development and justice, which are the exclusive preserve of the Nigerian state, the Federal Government.

When he is approached by Ebipade to provide their youth group with ammunition, Aswani ("The Whiteman" in the film) declares: "I'm here in the interest of my company; I am neither for your community nor for your country. I'm just a foreigner doing my own business to make my money." Slavoj Zizek notes in a similar vein how, "The fate of whole strata of the population and sometimes of whole countries can be decided by a 'solipsistic' speculative dance of capital, which pursues its goal of profitability in *blessed indifference* to how its movement will affect social reality".[299] Zizek analyses the ways in which capitalism flourishes within the operations of "systemic violence" in society. In a similar way, Aswani personifies this solipsistic performance of petrocapitalism in the way he demonstrates indifference to the crisis brewing around the operations of his business. He intervenes only when his business and personal safety come under direct threat by the local insurgency. This exemplifies the operational strategy of the oil extraction industry in the Niger Delta. Their interventions in the local crisis take the form of either a business strategy or a gesture of self-preservation. Since they pay royalties and taxes promptly into the secret accounts of government agents or private accounts of local compradors, chiefs or militants, these companies are not morally obliged to ensure that their business is beneficial to the host communities. The subtlety of this engagement in the film is remarkably different from the poetry studied in the previous chapters, especially in Bassey's text, which is unequivocal in calling out Big Oil and vilifying the ways in which the Niger Delta is exposed to unregulated and destructive modes of oil extraction.

Placing *Liquid Black* against a broader context of other cultural texts that index Petroculture, it is apparent that the film restricts itself to its immediate concerns of the realities affecting the ethical life of local communities in the Niger Delta. In contrast to this representative schema, we see a different narrative strategy unfold in the Hollywood film, *Syriana* (2006). The film captures the very web and weft of globalisation, the ways in which its operations across the globe generate discontents that are ramified in the lives of nations and peoples far flung across geographies and contexts. To think of the discontents of globalisation is to reflect on the problems and weaknesses of worldwide interconnections, and this is what *Syriana* portrays using oil as its signifying trope. At the centre of this globalised integration is an equally globalised resource – oil. By contrast, *Liquid Black* goes to the very heart of the provocation: the localised interstitial formations created to stoke violence as visible manifestations of all that is condemnable in how the extractive industry conducts business in the Niger Delta.

Conclusion

Liquid Black, then, is an allegory of the oil encounter in Nigeria. However, the film, like most Nollywood productions, heads for narrative closure, where every conflict is resolved, and the people live happily ever after. I think that a narrative such as the oil encounter, which resides in the discursive terrain of the unresolvable incoherencies, contradictions and paradoxes, should eschew closures, to prompt varied and alternative means of apprehending the crises occasioned by the oil politics in Nigeria. This is a techno-aesthetic glitch in Nollywood, and this makes the films excruciatingly predictable. If, as Imre Szeman notes, "Conclusions are suspended in order to better map the nervous system of oil capitalism", [300] it stands to reason that resistance in the context of oil extraction in Nigeria is an ongoing process with chains of events – mostly contradictory and paradoxical – co-occurring not in linear but in cyclical processes of incompleteness. This explains why Noel Carroll says that "The impression of completeness that makes for closure derives from our estimation…our pressing questions regarding the storyworld have been answered".[301] In reaching for narrative closure *The Liquid Black Gold* has seemed to bring some moral definition to the subject of violence in the region, insisting that, beyond the display of frenetic energy by the youth resource-rebels, there lies a desperate longing for an amicable and permanent solution to the Niger Delta crises. At any rate, the local communities in the Niger Delta are no doubt weary of conflicts. The longue durée of confrontation with the state and oil corporations has taken its toll on the ethical life of that region. Thus, implicit in the film's representation is a collective longing, or perhaps entreaty, for a permanent solution to the fraught encounter of oil in Nigeria.

Epilogue: Apocalyptic realism and the post-oil imagination in the Niger Delta

In the prologue to this book, where I reflect on the photographs in *Delta Remix: Last Rites Niger Delta,* I point to the combination of violence and ecological justice struggles in the representation of energy culture in postcolonial Nigeria. I propose a new interpretation of violence beyond its materially based response to the failure of governance and environmental pollution. Throughout this book, I have shown violence to be a metonymic device employed in the representations of the oil-resourced River Delta. Representation in this context becomes an operative term that extends or retracts legitimacy towards the thing it depicts, based on what it privileges. The images I reflect upon in the opening part of this book depict the militarised sociality of oil production and political ecology in the Niger Delta. In a sense, photographs are a form of imagistic and figurative language that requires interpretation; such images possess the ability to frame and encapsulate a story. Read in this way, photographs can also foreclose other stories or dimensions to a story that are not foregrounded in the image.[302] This book has therefore attempted to bring the elided aspects of the Niger Delta story into the enlarged frame of foregrounding and interpretation.

I now want to turn to a different set of images that envision the post-oil Niger Delta. These images gesture to an actuality of place *beyond* oil from which to engage climate discourse, depicting landscapes of devastation in apocalyptic proportions in the defunct sites of oil extraction. It is these textures of the real and the concrete that constitute what I call apocalyptic realism in the work of Zina Saro-Wiwa, the daughter of the slain environmental activist Ken Saro-Wiwa. Zina Saro-Wiwa (henceforth addressed simply as Zina) is a video artist, photographer and filmmaker. Her work features video installations, photographs and sound installations that stage performances related to everyday living, cultures, customs and traditions, and the environments of the Niger Delta, specifically the Ogoni.

In Zina's art, there is a manifest attempt to move away from oil and its troubled world of environmental devastation. In doing so, she stages performances of masquerades captured in photographs at the oil sites, as well as on top of decommissioned oil wellheads.[303] This is a powerful transgression of an otherwise restricted space, symbolising the end of the oil regime and a new beginning, in which the previous space of extraction is reconstituted into a place of quotidian existence – not only of the human but also of the extra- and nonhuman – and of testing new boundaries of ontology. In this way, Zina's art evinces how the local piece of earth, nature and all possibilities of life crumble under the sign of oil, bearing witness to the series of events that mark the culmination of the world's end. Yet, at the same time, thinking new regimes of energy requires a deliberate attempt to begin from the

Figure 3: *Still from Zina Saro-Wiwa, dir., 2015. Karikpo Pipeline, 5-channel digital video, 27 min.*

rubble of the incumbent regime of oil and to envision a world beyond oil, reading apocalyptic realism as an organising trope by which the end of the oil regime in the Delta is apprehended.

In short, Zina's art conceives new ways of being that are beyond the ken of modernity that the oil ontology inscribes in the Niger Delta. I use the term "beyond" precisely because the new world as imagined in these works emerges out of the aftermath of the one that attends oil extraction; her photographs do not eschew the usual ontologies of the real: environmental catastrophes, violence and other deprivations that mark the oil encounter in the Niger Delta. Rather, in foregrounding these negations, their harsh realities amplify and climax in an apocalyptic cadence. Nevertheless, out of this apocalyptic topos emerges a turning point in which an alternative world of oil's banishment comes into being. On Zina's website, it states that her installations "use folklore, masquerade traditions, religious practices, food and Nigerian popular aesthetics to test art's capacity to transform and to envision new concepts of environment and environmentalism".[304]

At centre stage in these eclectic performances is the defunct globalised infrastructure of oil extraction symbolised by the oil wellhead, which, in Nigeria's oil industry, is ironically (and cynically) called the "Christmas tree"– which is an object of beauty that shelters gifts and elicits joy in all who behold it. The trajectory of oil extraction in this place has left in its trail anything but gifts, and has elicited no joy in the communities that live in proximity to the oil installations, as witnessed, for instance, by the Ogoni affair, a subject that has attracted much scholarly attention.[305]

What this landscape evinces is the very *speech act* of paradox: a site with prodigious oil reserves and overwhelming social and ecological deprivations, a situation that, as I have made clear throughout this book, elicits a rich body of environmental writing and fashions a culture of militancy whose politics of resistance exacerbates the issues it purports to address.

One figure who embodies this incongruous relation of oil extraction, non-violent resistance and violence is Zina's famous father, Ken Saro-Wiwa. In his lifetime, he succeeded in challenging, with remarkable effect, the state's authority over oil revenue and environmental despoliation. Despite using non-violent strategies of cultural protests and imaginative writing, he met with a tragic death at the hands of the Nigerian government. Perhaps then, categorising the paradox of the "Christmas Tree" as a metaphor of lived reality does not do complete justice to the workings of paradox in this oilscape. Paradox bears out in insidious and tangible ways in the Niger Delta.

The Christmas tree wellhead in Zina's art is presented, on the one hand, as a monument to human hubris, consigned to the past, never to be fetishised again. On the other hand, it is also a heuristic device for rethinking the emergence of a new ontology in which oil extraction exhausts its purchase and is discontinued and consigned to history. The locality of its extraction is thus reclaimed and reconstituted into a place of being. The site of the wellhead, which used to be a territorialised space of enclosure, protected and enclaved, becomes instead a playground for the local community: a place where they can lose themselves in a new sense of being and self-ownership; a chance to reinvent ways of being local, and to re-establish a relationship with their culture. In fact, the site of the decommissioned wellhead becomes one for experimenting with a new lease of being, of a non human-centred sociality. It becomes a site where one can commune with the environment, in a world where deities, spirits, animals, humans and other cosmic beings can constellate without the intrusion of the disruptive modernity that oil extraction perpetuated in that locality.

Chakrabarty has noted that "postcolonial studies at this historical juncture must have to confront two imperatives of our time: globalization and global warming".[306] Zina's art is playful but consciously organised to rehabilitate and re-inhabit the landscape, which, hitherto, had been given to oil extraction. The local landscape, once demarcated for the exclusive purpose of oil extraction, is repopulated with the presence of mythical creatures, deities, ancestral masquerades and the human, all constellating around an object that hitherto was completely territorialised. Thus, Zina is de-globalising the landscape of oil extraction in Ogoniland.

In his widely cited essay, "At the Edge of the World: Boundaries, Territoriality, and Sovereignty in Africa", Achille Mbembe provides a fascinating analysis of how territorial formations in Africa domesticate globalisation into what he calls, drawing on Heidegger and Fernand Braudel, "world time".[307] Mbembe discusses this world time as the peculiar configuration of space and time in the operations of globalisation in Africa, organised to control spaces and resources, and, in the process, "proceeds in the material deconstruction of existing territorial framework", excising "conventional boundaries" and simultaneously creating "spaces of enclosure intended to limit the mobility" of local populations adjudged "superfluous".[308] It is this notion of local superfluity that Zina's art is challenging by engaging the territoriality of oil extraction in a playful act of occupation, bringing their excess of being into the very stage where the Anthropocene is most visible: the globalised infrastructure of oil in the Niger Delta.

Zina renders the symbol of that globalised infrastructure, the oil wellhead, provincial by suffusing it with local characters and turning its surrounding plain into a playground for these beings. I read this as a powerful mode of transgressing the global and of envisioning a way out of an impasse that orients towards oil – that "hyperobject"[309] of modernity's will and desire – for which there appears to be no alternative. Zina's is an attempt to reconfigure new possibilities of life that decentre the one built around fossil fuel, unconditioned by instrumentality and thoroughly idiosyncratic, as is often the case with new beginnings.

In her attempt to envision a new beginning beyond the world of fossil-fuelled modernity, Zina has artfully domesticated a space previously internationalised, reconfiguring the landscape as a space ontologically charged with the quotidian, where one could play and be at ease. Notice also the mask worn by the performer. It represents a local Ogoni deity; possibly no longer in fashion, or at least not after those dark days of the Ogoni people's struggles with the Nigerian state. Zina uses cultural artefacts, such as masquerades, to challenge the form of globalism by which the international infrastructure of oil extraction operates. Indeed, the image of the masquerade as depicted in Zina's art is not new. The masquerade is both a material image of culture as well as metaphorical in nature. In his time, Ken Saro-Wiwa also employed the image of the masquerade in his creative work, to great effect. In his polemic, A Month and A Day (1995), Saro-Wiwa describes the comprador petty bourgeoisie as "black colonialists who wear the mask of Nigerianism", who in truth are "masquerades leashed to a rope held by an unseen hand, and steadied by the oil of the Ogoni and other peoples in the Niger Delta".[310] Therefore, perhaps reclaiming and re-appropriating the image of the masquerade into an agent for good is a useful way of signalling the end of the oil regime and generating a productive future out of that terrible history. In Zina's art, such cultural artefacts are rehabilitated and restored, to once again feature at the centre of cultural life, but this time in ways more positive and generative. What we find, therefore, is a simultaneous constellation of the past, present and future. It is a re-memory, not of "the transnational oil culture that has been overwhelmingly identified with Ogoniland",[311] but rather a memory that precedes all that the wider world (read as Euro-American) knows about the Niger Delta. In a sense, while her art constitutes a drive towards a future imagined in a post-extraction society, it is indeed also a re-inscription of the past that precedes oil extraction. What the artist appears to suggest is that any attempt to think a way out of the current regime of oil extraction and dependence must not be divorced from the place of knowing, of the quotidian, of culture, where one is grounded both constitutionally and historically. And so, her art is a performance that comes with a caveat, which is that an attempt to reach for the new must not yield completely to this new – the abstract or the ostensibly scientific – but must bring into the fray something valuable from the past as a means of reconstituting the collective future.

Assembling human and nonhuman characters around the decommissioned oil wellhead is indexical of an awakening to a new regime of vision. Stephanie LeMenager, in a similar reading of the images calls this a "sociability – being together for the sake of being alive together", implying "playfulness, creative and open thinking".[312] Zina's vision is thus alert to the limitations of the human who, in his/her sterile politics, often pretends to rational and scientific solutions to global warming, where none is afoot. This is the reason why Zina tropes on the otherwise nonsensical and the playful, as a necessary starting point from which to imagine new horizons of possibility. It is also an attempt to recuperate and reconfigure this specific space as a place of everyday, commonplace existence for all beings, rather than a fetishised space of commodity extraction. Zina's art embodies the practice of an ethical code that is sympathetic to the culture and history of this troubled petroleumscape, and that runs through almost all the texts assembled for analysis in this book. This overarching ethical code demonstrated in the texts permeates conceptions of human and nonhuman in the throes of violent exactions, rendering these categories indistinguishable and levelling binaries that might otherwise separate them.

About the author

Philip Aghoghovwia is a senior lecturer in the Department of English at the University of the Free State (UFS). He has been a fellow or awardee of several prestigious organisations, including the African Humanities Program of the American Council of Learned Societies funded by the Carnegie Corporation of New York; the Department of Higher Education and Training (DHET) Future Professors Programme; and the UFS Future Generation Professoriate. Aghoghovwia holds a Y1 rating from the National Research Fund (NRF). His research is in environmental humanities, African literature, energy and water studies, and the cultures and politics of resource extraction in Africa. His recent essays have appeared in *English Academy Review* (2020), *Climate Realism: The Aesthetics of Weather and Atmosphere in the Anthropocene* (Routledge, 2020), *South African Journal of Science* (2021), *Safundi* (2021), *Interventions* (2021), *Nature and Literary Studies* (Cambridge University Press, 2022) and *Social Dynamics* (2022).

Notes

1   Christine Stelzig, Eva Ursprung and Stefan Eisenhofer, eds. *Last Rites Niger Delta: The Drama of Oil Production in Contemporary Photographs* (Munich: Staatliches Museum fur Volkerkunde Munchen, 2012).

2   The exhibition was curated by Zen Marie and other colleagues at the Wits School of Arts, the University of the Witwatersrand. It was part of a series of events at the Johannesburg Workshop in Theory and Criticism (JWTC) in the winter of 2012.

3   Judith Butler, *Gender Trouble: Feminism and the Subversion of Identity* (New York: Routledge, 1990), 1.

4   Rob Nixon, *Slow Violence and the Environmentalism of the Poor* (Cambridge: Harvard University Press, 2011).

5   Michael Watts, "Blood Oil: The Anatomy of a Petro-Insurgency in the Niger Delta, Nigeria", in *Crude Domination: An Anthology of Oil,* eds Andrea Berhrends and Stephen P Reyna (New York: Berghan Books, 2011), 62.

6   Nixon, 15.

7   Edward Said, "Opponents, Audiences, Constituencies, and Community", *Critical Inquiry,* vol. 9, no. 1 (1982), 24–25.

8   Ken Saro-Wiwa, *Genocide in Nigeria: The Ogoni Tragedy* (Port Harcourt: Saros International, 1992), 36.

9   I have in mind the state-sanctioned execution of Saro-Wiwa by General Sani Abacha, and the new grammar of violence that has come to achieve salience both in the social world of the Delta and in the aesthetic tropes of artistic representations of the oil encounter in this region. I argue that these conjunctures give a special evocation – an eerie one – to Paul Anderson's film title, *There Will Be Blood* (dir. Paul Thomas Anderson; perf. Daniel Day-Lewis and Paul Dano, 2007. DVD). The film is an adaptation of Upton Sinclair's novel, *Oil!,* a fictional story of the discovery of oil and the capitalist ethos of individualism, ambition, greed, and violence that shape the ontology of oil since its discovery in nineteenth-century United States of America.

10 This notion is to be found in Adewale Meja-Pearce's two controversial essays on Ken Saro-Wiwa. The first, "Feed the Charm" published 25 July 2002 (*London Review of Books*, vol. 24, no. 14: 23–26), is a review of Ken Wiwa's memoir of his father: *In the Shadow of a Saint: A Son's Journey to Understand His Father's Legacy* (Toronto: Penguin Random House Canada, 2000). The other, more scathing and perhaps snide, is to be found in Meja-Pearce's book of essays, *Remembering Ken Saro-Wiwa and Other Essays* (Lagos: The New Gong, 2005). See, especially, pages 9–48.

11 See Ed Pilkington, "Shell Pays Out $15.5m over Saro-Wiwa Killing", *The Guardian*, Tuesday, 9 June 2009. http://www.guardian.co.uk/world/2009/jun/08/nigeria-usa.

12 Chinyere Nwahunanya, "Introduction: From Boom to Doom – The Niger Delta in Contemporary Nigerian Literature", in *From Boom to Doom: Protest and Conflict Resolutions in the Literature of the Niger Delta*, ed. Chinyere Nwahunanya (Owerri: Springfield Publishers, 2011), xiv.

13 Godini Darah, "Revolutionary Pressures in Niger Delta Literatures", in *From Boom to Doom*, 12.

14 Jennifer Wenzel, *The Disposition of Nature: Environmental Crisis and World Literature* (New York: Fordham University Press, 2020). According to Wenzel, Nigerian literary creative boom (and eventual, if temporal, decline) followed the contours of the Nigerian oil boom and bust: oil was first exported out of Nigeria in 1958, the same year in which Chinua Achebe's debut novel – and Nigeria's seminal literary export – *Things Fall Apart* was published in London. The flourishing of literary creativity in Nigeria that followed Achebe's novel overlaps with the Nigerian oil boom and the wealth that flowed into the country in the 1960s and 1970s. Thus "the crash of the global oil market and the Nigerian economy in the 1980s was followed by a significant decline" in the literary output coming out of Nigeria during this time (88–89).

15 Wenzel, 118, 129.

16 Wenzel, 88–89, *passim*. (Italics in original).

17 Darah, 13.

18 Nwahunanya, xviii.

19 See, for instance, Nollywood video films such as *The Liquid Black Gold* (2010), which I discuss in Chapter 4, *Crude War* (2010) and *The Amnesty* (2011), all written, produced and directed by the same individuals using virtually the same cast. There is also the film *Black November* (2012), a Hollywood collaboration and titled in commemoration of the November execution of Saro-Wiwa and the Ogoni Eight. The film is directed by the Nigerian-born Jetta Amata.

20 Nduka Otiono shared this very interesting point in a panel discussion at the Petrocultures Conference, where he presented a paper with the title "Saro-Wiwa's Ghost: The Niger Delta Struggle and Nollywood Filmic Representation" (Petrocultures: Oil, Energy, Cultures Conference, University of Alberta, Canada, 9 September 2012.).

21 See, inter alia, Cyril Obi and Siri Rustad, eds. *Oil and Insurgency in the Niger Delta* (Uppsala: Nordic Africa Institute, 2011); Eghosa Osaghae, "The Ogoni Uprising", *African Affairs*, vol. 95 (1995): 325–344; Tom Burgis, *The Looting Machine* (London: William Collins, 2016); and Michael Watts, "Petro-Insurgency or Criminal Syndicate?", *Review of African Political Economy*, vol. 114 (2007): 637–660.

22 See James Tsaaior, "Poetics, Politics and the Paradoxes of Oil in Nigeria's Niger Delta Region", *African Renaissance*, vol. 2, no. 6 (2005): 72–80; Ogaga Okuyade, "The Cumulative Neglect of Collective Responsibility: Postcoloniality, Ecology, and the Niger Delta", *Matatu*, vol. 39, no. 7 (2011): 115–131; and Tanure Ojaide and Enajite Ojaruega, eds. *The Literature and Arts of the Niger Delta* (New York: Routledge, 2021).

23 Amitav Ghosh, "Petrofiction: The Oil Encounter and the Novel". This essay was originally published in 1992 as a review of *The Cities of Salt Trilogy* published in 1989 by the Jordanian writer Abdelrahman Munif. However, the version cited here appears in Ghosh's collection of essays, *The Imam and the Indian* (New Delhi: Ravi Dayal Publisher, 2002).

24 Ghosh, 76.

25 Ghosh, 79.

26 In *The Great Derangement: Climate Change and the Unthinkable* (University of Chicago

Press, 2016), Ghosh made similar claims regarding the crisis of a literary form that is adequate to the seriousness and grandness of the phenomenon at hand, in this case, the global climate crisis. Ghosh frames this reprised reflection "a crisis of culture and a poverty of the collective imagination" (9) – a nod to the book's title, *The Great Derangement* –that is, our collective inability to account for the extant dimensions of oil modernity and its planetary impacts.

27 See James Ferguson, *Global Shadows: Africa in the Neoliberal World Order* (Durham: Duke University Press, 2006); and Achille Mbembe, "Footnotes on the Offshore City".,*The Johannesburg Salon*, no. 7 (2014): 142–143.

28 Ferguson, 195.

29 See Philip Aghoghovwia, "Is the Anthropocene Conniving with Capital? Water Priva(tisa) tion and Ontology Reimagined in Karen Jayes' For the Mercy of Water", *Interventions* (2021): 4. Retrieved from: https://doi.org/10.1080/1369801X.2021.2015704.

30 See Andrew H. Apter, *The Pan-African Nation: Oil and the Spectacle of Culture in Nigeria* (Chicago: University of Chicago Press, 2005); or, more explicitly, Michael Ross, *The Oil Curse* (Princeton: Princeton University Press, 2012).

31 Stephanie LeMenager, "Eden if We Dare", in *Did You Know We Taught Them How to Dance?*. An exhibition catalogue on the work of Zina Saro-Wiwa (Houston: Blaffer Art Museum, University of Houston, 2016), 39.

32 Byron Caminero-Santangelo, *Different Shades of Green* (Charlottesville: University of Virginia Press, 2014), 32.

33 Paul Crutzen and Eugene Stoermer, "The Anthropocene", *IGPB (International Geosphere-Biosphere Programme) Newsletter,* no. 41 (May 2000): 17–18.

34 Elmar Altvater, "The Capitalocene, or, Geoengineering against Capitalism's Planetary Boundaries", in *Anthropocene or Capitalocene? Nature, History, and the Crisis of Capitalism*, ed. Jason Moore (Oakland: Kairos, 2016), 138–152.

35 Crutzen and Stoermer, 17; see also Jan Zalasiewicz, Mark Williams, Will Steffen and Paul Crutzen, "The New World of Anthropocene", *Environmental Science & Technology*, vol. 44, no. 7 (2010): 2228–2231.

36 See, inter alia, Paul Crutzen, "Geology of Mankind: the Anthropocene", *Nature*, no. 415 (2002): 22–23; Will Steffen, "The Anthropocene". Filmed 4 November, 2010 in Canberra, Australia. TEDx video, 18:15. Retrieved from: https://youtu.be/ABZjlfhN0EQ; Dipesh Chakrabarty, "History on an Expanded Canvas: The Anthropocene's Invitation". Keynote speech presented at *The Anthropocene Project: An Opening*, Haus der Kulturen de Welt, Berlin, 13 January 2013. Retrieved from: https://youtu.be/svgqLPFpaOg; and Eileen Crist, "On the Poverty of Our Nomenclature", in *Anthropocene or Capitalocene?*, ed. Jason Moore (Oakland: Kairos, 2016), 14–33.

37 Paul Crutzen and Will Steffen, "How Long Have We Been in the Anthropocene Era?", *Climate Change* vol. 63, no. 3 (2003): 251–257; Dipesh Chakrabarty, "Anthropocene 1", in *Fueling Culture: 101 Words for Energy and Environment*, eds. Imre Szeman, Jennifer Wenzel, and Patricia Yaeger (New York: Fordham University Press, 2017), 39–42.

38 See Will Steffen, "The Anthropocene: Where on Earth Are We Going?". Keynote speech presented at *The Anthropocene Project: An Opening*, Haus der Kulturen de Welt, Berlin,

10 January, 2013. Retrieved from: https://youtu.be/T8U6y4UNXRQ; Timothy Morton, *Hyperobjects: Philosophy and Ecology after the End of the World* (Minneapolis: University of Minnesota Press, 2013); and Noam Chomsky, "The Anthropocene, 6th Extinction, and Climate Change". Lecture presented at St Olaf College, USA, 6 May 2018. Retrieved from: https://youtu.be/kjIsuGHdbnw.

39   Crist, 24.

40   Crist, 14.

41   Jason Moore, ed., *Anthropocene or Capitalocene? Nature, History, and the Crisis of Capitalism* (Oakland: Kairos, 2016).

42   Naomi Klein, *This Changes Everything: Capitalism vs The Climate* (New York: Simon & Schuster, 2014), 18.

43   Klein, 22.

44   Chakrabarty, "Anthropocene 1", 41.

45   Chakrabarty, 42.

46   See Rob Nixon, "Anthropocene 2", in *Fueling Culture: 101 Words for Energy and Environment*, eds. Imre Szeman, Jennifer Wenzel and Patricia Yaeger (New York: Fordham University Press, 2017), 43–46; and Klein 2014, 1–28.

47   Chakrabarty, 42.

48   Jean-Paul Sartre, "Preface" to *Wretched of the Earth*, by Frantz Fanon (London: Penguin, 1961), 7.

49   Nixon, "Anthropocene 2", 44.

50   Dipesh Chakrabarty 2013; Chomsky 2018.

51   Timothy Mitchell, "Carbon Democracy", *Economy and Society*, vol. 38, no. 3 (2009): 400.

52   Steffen, "The Anthropocene".

53   Some of the reasons for this misalignment are discussed in detail in Philip Aghoghovwia's "Postcolonial Nature", in *Nature and Literary Studies*, eds, Peter Remien and Scott Slovic (Cambridge: Cambridge University Press, forthcoming)

54   See Nixon, *Slow Violence*; Caminero-Santangelo 2014; Cajetan Iheka, *Naturalizing Africa: Ecological Violence, Agency, and Postcolonial Resistance in African Literature* (Cambridge: Cambridge University Press, 2018); and Louise Green, *Fragments from the History of Loss: The Nature Industry and the Postcolony* (State College, PA: Pennsylvania State University Press, 2020).

55   Nixon, 2–10.

56   Ramachandra Guha and Juan Martinez-Alier, *Varieties of Environmentalism: Essays North and South* (London: Earthscan, 1997).

57   Caminero-Santangelo, 189, 170.

58   Iheka, 3.

59   Iheka, 22–23.

60   Iheka, 85.

61   Iheka, 23.

62   Iheka, 106.

63 Timothy Morton, *The Ecological Thought* (Cambridge: Harvard University Press, 2010), 8; quoted in Iheka, 106.

64 Iheka, 107.

65 Iheka, 125.

66 See Graham Huggan and Helen Tiffin, *Postcolonial Ecocriticism: Literature, Animals, Environment* (New York: Routledge, 2010); Pablo Mukherjee, *Postcolonial Environments, Nature, Culture, and the Contemporary Indian Novel in English* (New York: Palgrave, 2010); Iheka 2018; to name just a few.

67 Iheka, 85–125.

68 See Sunny Awhefeada, "Degraded Environment and Destabilized Women in Kaine Agary's *Yellow-Yellow*", in *Eco-Critical Literature: Regreening African Landscapes*, ed. Ogaga Okuyade (New York: African Heritage Press, 2013), 95–108; and Charles Feghabo, "Inverting Otherness in Kaine Agary's *Yellow-Yellow*", *Matatu*, no. 45 (2014): 315–332.

69 Sule Egya, "Literary Militancy and Helon Habila's *Oil on Water*", *Research in African Literatures*, vol. 48, no. 4 (2017): 94–104; and Senayon Olaoluwa, "Dislocating Anthropocene: The City and Oil in Helon Habila's *Oil on Water*", *ISLE: Interdisciplinary Studies in Literature and Environment*, vol. 27, no. 2 (2020): 243–267.

70 Iheka, 125.

71 Egya, "Literary Militancy" 94, 97.

72 Basil Nnamdi, Obari Gomba and Frank Ugiomoh, "Environmental Challenges and Eco-Aesthetics in Nigeria's Niger Delta", *Third Text*, vol. 27, no. 1 (2013): 65–75.

73 David Goldberg, "Epistemologies of Deception: Topologies of the Extra/Ordinary", *The Johannesburg Salon*, no. 5 (2012), 56.

74 John Pepper Clark, *The Raft* (London: Oxford University Press, 1964), 16.

75 Louise Green, "The Aphorism and the Historical Image: Adorno's Politics of Form", *The Johannesburg Salon*, no. 5 (2012): 80-85.

76 Clark, *The Raft*, 1964.

77 Giogio Agambem, *Homo Sacer: Sovereign Power and Bare Life*, trans. Daniel Heller Roazen (Paolo Alto: Stanford University Press, 1998).

78 Ebi Yeibo, *A Song for Tomorrow* (Ibadan: Kraftgriots, 2003), 18.

79 Yeibo, 15–60; 81-87.

80 Mikhail Bakhtin, *Speech Genres & Other Late Essays*, eds. Caryl Emerson and Michael Holsquist (Austin: University of Texas Press, 2004), 33.

81 Bakhtin, 36.

82 Bakhtin, 34–35.

83 Yeibo, 18.

84 Yeibo, 18.

85 Yeibo, 18.

86 Yeibo, 18.

87 Genesis 6: 5–22.

88 Yeibo, 18.

89   Yeibo, 11.

90   Yeibo, 18.

91   Fátima Vieira, "The Concept of Utopia", in *The Cambridge Companion to Utopian Literature*, ed. Gregory Claeys (Cambridge: Cambridge University Press, 2010), 17.

92   Yeibo, 18.

93   Vieira, 17–23.

94   Yeibo, 33.

95   Niyi Osundare, *Dialogue With My Country* (Ibadan: Bookcraft, 2007), 155.

96   Robert Fulford, *The Triumph of the Narrative* (Toronto: Anansi, 1999), 95.

97   Fulford, 97.

98   Bakhtin, *Speech Genres & Other Late Essays,* 15.

99   See for instance JP Clark, *The Raft* (London: Oxford University Press, 1964).

100 Yeibo, 20.

101 Yeibo, 20.

102 Yeibo, 25.

103 Yeibo, 25.

104 Yeibo, 25–26.

105 Yeibo, 83.

106 Yeibo, 84.

107 Quoted in Sunny Awhefeada, "History and the Politics of Representation in the Postcolonial African Text", in *Politics of the Postcolonial Text,* ed. James Tsaaior (Munich: Lincom Europa, 2010), 180.

108 Ato Quayson, *Calibrations: Reading for the Social* (Minneapolis: University of Minnesota Press, 2003), 150.

109 Nnimmo Bassey, *To Cook a Continent: Destructive Extraction and the Climate Crisis in Africa* (Cape Town: Pambazuka Press, 2012), 1.

110 *Democracy Now: A Daily Independent TV/Radio Global News Hour Program with Amy Goodman and Juan Gonzalez.* Rio de Janeiro, Thursday, 21 June 2012. http://www. democracynow.org.

111 See Nnimmo Bassey, "Leave it in the Ground", *New Internationalist,* vol. 419, no. 1 (2009). Retrieved from: https://newint.org/features/2009/01/01/climate-justice-bassey-evans.

112 Patrick Bond, *Politics of Climate Justice: Paralysis above, Movement Below* (Durban: University of KwaZulu-Natal Press, 2012), 205.

113 L. Temper, I. Yánez, K. Sharife, O. Godwin and J. Martinez-Alier, *Towards a Post-Oil Civilization, Yasunization and Other Initiatives to Leave Fossil Fuels in the Soil.* EJOLT Report no. 6, 2013, 6.

114 For a detailed discussion of this subject, see Pamela L. Martin, "Global Governance from the Amazon: Leaving Oil Underground in Yasuni National Park, Ecuador", *Global Environmental Politics,* vol. 11, no. 4 (2011): 22–42.

115 In an interview with Vanessa Baird, "Arts: The Bard of Environmental Justice Speaks", *New Internationalist* (December 2011): 39–40.

116 Baird, 39.

117 Graham Huggan, "'Greening' Postcolonialism: Ecocritical Perspectives", *Modern Fiction Studies*, vol. 58, no. 3 (2004): 703.

118 Val Plumwood, *Environmental Culture: The Ecological Crisis of Reason* (London: Routledge, 2001).

119 Graham Huggan and Helen Tiffin, 4–5

120 Bassey, *We Thought It Was Oil* (Ibadan: Kraftgriots, 2002), 14–15

121 Bassey, 15.

122 Sule Egya, "Eco-Human Engagement in Recent Nigerian Poetry in English", *Journal of Postcolonial Writing*, vol. 49, no. 1 (2013): 64.

123 Oyeniyi Okunoye, "Writing Resistance: Dissidence and Visions of Healing in Nigerian Poetry of the Military Era", *Tydskrif vir letterkunde*, vol. 48, no. 1 (2011): 71.

124 Bassey, *We Thought It Was Oil*, 16. (Italics in original.)

125 Bassey, 16–7.

126 Greg Garrard, *Ecocriticism: The New Critical Idiom* (London: Routledge, 2004), 99.

127 Harry Garuba, "Ken Saro-Wiwa's *Sozaboy* and the Logic of Minority Discourse", in *Ogoni Agonies: Ken Saro-Wiwa and the Crises in Nigeria*, ed. Abdul-Rasheed Na-Allah (New York: Africa World Press, 1998), 229. (Italics in the original.)

128 Bassey, *We Thought It Was Oil*, 29. (Italics in the original.)

129 Jay Parini, *Why Poetry Matters* (New Haven: Yale University Press, 2008), xii.

130 Dipesh Chakrabarty, "Where is the Now?", *Critical Inquiry* vol. 30, no. 2 (2004): 459.

131 Chakrabarty, 459; 462.

132 Bassey, *We Thought It Was Oil*, 28.

133 Nixon, 4.

134 Bassey, 28.

135 Bassey, 28.

136 Bassey, 28.

137 Nnimmo Bassey, "A Movement is Not a Bicycle Wheel." Speech delivered at a Town Hall Meeting on Fracking and Shell Petroleum Company, Liberty Hall Theatre, Dublin, 21 June 2012. Retrieved from: https://www.youtube.com/watch?v=TDSnsprGUj0

138 Nixon, 235.

139 Quoted in Huggan and Tiffin, 13.

140 Huggan and Tiffin, 13.

141 Huggan and Tiffin, 13–14.

142 See Pius Adesanmi and Chris Dunton, "Nigeria's Third Generation Writing: Historiography and Preliminary Theoretical Considerations", *English in Africa*, vol. 32, no. 1 (2005): 7–19; and Harry Garuba, "The Unbearable Lightness of Being: Re-figuring Trends in Recent Nigerian Poetry", *English in Africa*, vol. 32, no. 1 (2005): 51–72; and Sule Egya, *Nation, Power and Dissidence in Third-Generation Nigerian Poetry in English* (Pretoria: UNISA Press, 2014).

143 Adesanmi and Dunton, 9.

144 Egya, *Nation*, 6.

145 Egya, 2.

146 Egya, 140.

147 Agambem, 1998.

148 The source for the Prometheus legend is unknown. However, it is credited to Aeschylus, said to have written a trilogy of plays about Prometheus's theft of fire, only one of which survives as *The Promethean Bound*. The version I draw from here is the English translation by James George Frazer, published in Vol. 1, *Loeb Classical Library*, eds. TE Page and WHT Rouse (London: William Heinemann, 1921).

149 Northrop Frye, "Preface", in *The Psychoanalysis of Fire*, by Gaston Bachelard (London: Routledge, 1964), vi.

150 Gaston Bachelard, *The Psychoanalysis of Fire* (London: Routledge, 1964), 7–21.

151 Jeffrey Cohen and Lowell Duckert, *Elemental Ecocriticism: Thinking with Earth, Air, Water and Fire* (Minneapolis: University of Minnesota Press, 2015), 4.

152 Cohen and Duckert, 4–5.

153 Anne Harris, "Pyromena Fire's Doing" in *Elemental Ecocriticism: Thinking with Earth, Air, Water and Fire*, eds. Jeffrey Cohen and Lowell Duckert (Minneapolis: University of Minnesota Press, 2015), 47.

154 Mildred Mortimer, *Writing from the Hearth: Public, Domestic and Imaginative Space in Francophone Women's Fiction of Africa and the Caribbean* (Minneapolis: Lexington Books, 2007), 71.

155 See Oladotun Ayobade, "Women That Danced the Fire Dance: Fela Kuti's Afrobeat Queens, Performance and the Dialectics of Postcolonial Identity". Unpublished PhD Diss., University of Texas at Austin, 2016.

156 Ogaga Ifowodo, *The Oil Lamp* (Trenton: Africa World Press, 2005). The name of the community spells as "Jesse", but it would seem that Ifowodo has taken poetic liberty by spelling with a single "s" in the poem. Throughout this essay, I shall preserve the integrity of his poetic license by retaining the single "s" when referencing the poem; and I will use the double "s" in reference to the local community of Jesse.

157 Ike Okonta and Oronto Douglas, *Where Vultures Feast: Shell, Human Rights and Oil in the Niger Delta* (New York: Verso, 2003), 196.

158 Naomi Klein, "Let Them Drown: The Violence of Othering in a Warming World", *London Review of Books*, vol 38, no. 11 (2016): 11–14.

159 Senayon Olaoluwa, "Dislocating Anthropocene: The City and Oil in Helon Habila's *Oil on Water*", *ISLE: Interdisciplinary Studies in Literature and Environment*, vol. 27, no. 2 (2020): 257.

160 See the United Nations Environment Programme's *Environmental Assessment of Ogoniland Report,* 2011. Retrieved from: https://www.unep.org/explore-topics/disasters-conflicts/where-we-work/nigeria/environmental-assessment-ogoniland-report; and the Amnesty International Publications on Nigeria, titled *Bad information: Oil spill investigations in the Niger Delta*, 2013. Retrieved from: https://www.amnesty.org/en/documents/afr44/028/2013/en/

161 Quoted in Iheka, 111–112.

162 Iheka, 111.

163 See, inter alia, Michael Watts, "Resource Curse? Governmentality, Oil and Power in the Niger Delta, Nigeria", *Geopolitics,* vol. 9, no. 1 (2004): 50–80.

164 Harris, 28.

165 Caminero-Santangelo, 170.

166 Egya, *Nation,* 149.

167 Ifowodo, 7–8.

168 Hilary Anderson, "Hundreds of People Burned to Death in Southern Nigeria", *BBC Online News Report,* 19 October 1998.

169 Tony Jupiter, "The Jesse Fire Disaster". *BBC Online,* 19 October 1998.

170 Ifowodo, 7.

171 Toni Morrison, "The Site of Memory", in *Inventing the Truth: The Art and Craft of Memoir,* ed. William Zinsser (Boston: Houghton Mifflin, 1995), 87.

172 Morrison, 91.

173 Ifowodo, 9.

174 Mikhail Bakhtin, "Carnival Ambivalence", *The Bakhtin Reader: Selected Writings of Bakhtin, Medvedev and Voloshinov,* edited by Pam Morris (London: Arnold Publishers, 1994), 194–244.

175 Caminero-Santangelo, 179.

176 Morrison, 93.

177 Ifowodo, 5.

178 Ifowodo, 5.

179 Douglas Kaze, "The Environmental Imagination in Arthur Nortje's Poetry". Unpublished PhD Diss., Rhodes University, 2018, p. 152.

180 Quoted in Ifowodo, iii.

181 Ifowodo, 11.

182 Ifowodo, 13.

183 Ifowodo, 8.

184 Caminero-Santangelo, 177.

185 Ifowodo, 8.

186 Ifowodo, 15.

187 Mikhail Bakhtin, *Rabelais and His World,* trans. Helene Iswolsky (Bloomington: Indiana University Press, 1984).

188 Bakhtin, *Rabelais* 10.

189 Ifowodo, 21.

190 Ifowodo, 21.

191 Terry Eagleton, *How to Read a Poem* (London: Blackwell Publishing, 2007), 6.

192 Ifowodo, 21.

193 Ifowodo, 21.

194 Egya, *Nation* 7.

195 Egya, 7.

196 Judith Butler, *Precarious Life: The Power of Mourning and Violence* (New York: Verso, 2004), 155.

197 Garuba, 65.

198 Ifowodo, 5.

199 Frantz Fanon, *Wretched of the Earth.* (London: Penguin, 1961), 203.

200 Emmanuel Obiechina, "Poetry as Therapy: Reflections on Achebe's "Christmas in Biafra" and Other Poems", *Callaloo*, vol. 25, no. 2 (2002), 530.

201 Francis Wheen, *Mumbo-Jumbo* (London: Harper Perennial, 2004), 68.

202 Lewis Nkosi, *Tasks and Masks: Themes and Styles of African Literature* (Essex: Longman, 1981), 31.

203 Tanure Ojaide, "I Want to Be an Oracle: My Poetry and My Generation", *World Literature Today*, vol. 68, no. 1 (1994): 15–21.

204 Ojaide, 15.

205 Gross National Product.

206 Uzoechi Nwagbara, "Poetics of Resistance: Ecocitical Reading of Ojaide's Delta Blues and Daydream of Ants", *African Study Monographs*, vol. 31, no. 1 (2010): 17.

207 Funso Aiyejina, "Recent Nigerian Poetry in English: An Alter/native Tradition". *Perspectives on Nigerian Literature 1700 to the Present* (Lagos: Guardian Publishing, 1988), 124.

208 See Chinweizu, Onwuchekwa Jemie and Ihechukwu Madubuike, *Toward the Decolonization of African Literature. Vol. 1: African Fiction and Poetry and Their Critics* (Enugu: Fourth Dimension Publishers, 1980).

209 Stephanie Newell, *West African Literatures: Ways of Reading* (Oxford: Oxford University Press, 2006), 131.

210 Newell, 132.

211 Tanuré Ojaide, *Delta Blues & Home Songs* (Ibadan: Kraft Books, 1998), 12.

212 Ojaide, 13.

213 Ojaide, 21.

214 Ojaide, 21–22.

215 Charles Bodunde, "Tanure Ojaide's Poetry and the Delta Landscape: A Study of *Delta Blues & Home Songs*", in *Writing the Homeland: The Poetry and Politics of Tanure Ojaide,* ed. Onookome Okome (Bayreuth: Bayreuth African Studies, 2002), 201.

216 Ojaide, *Delta Blues,* 17–18.

217 Ojaide, 17.

218 Ojaide, 18.

219 Quoted in Ogaga Okuyade, "The Cumulative Neglect of Collective Responsibility: Postcoloniality and Ecology in the Poetry of Tanure Ojaide", *Matatu,* vol. 39, no. 7 (2011): 124.

220 Ojaide, "I Want To Be an Oracle", 21.

221 Ojaide, *Delta Blues,* 19.

222 Ojaide, 25.

223 Ojaide, 41.

224 Ilan Stavans, "Is American Literature Parochial?", *World Literature Today,* vol. 87, no. 4 (July 2013): 29.

225 Fanon, 150.

226 Fanon, 205.

227 Abuja is the capital city of Nigeria, a post-civil war creation of the federal military government of Murtala Mohammed in 1976, built from the immense wealth that the 1970s oil boom had brought to Nigeria. The money, which could have helped to develop vital sectors of the country's weak economy, and to cushion the effect of pollution the oil exploration had brought on the Niger Delta environment, was used instead to build a brand-new city for the vainglory of Nigeria's political elites. Abuja exemplifies the postcolonial extravagance and self-serving interests that seem to define politics and leadership in Nigeria.

228 Nixon, *Slow Violence,* 19.

229 Nixon, 19.

230 Tijan Sallah, "The Eagle's Vision: the Poetry of Tanure Ojaide", *Research in African Literatures,* vol. 26, no. 1 (1995): 21.

231 Oyeniyi Okunoye, "Alterity, Marginality and the National Question in the Poetry of the Niger Delta." *Cahiers d'etudes Africaines,* vol 48, no. 191 (2008): 416.

232 Bakhtin, *The Bakhtin Reader* 113.

233 Mikhail Bakhtin, "Literary Stylistics: The Construction of the Utterance". *Bakhtin School Papers,* trans. Noel Owen (Oxford: Oxford University Press, 1987), 114–115.

234 Bakhtin, "Literary Stylistics", 118–119.

235 Mikhail Bakhtin, *The Dialogic Imagination: Four Essays,* ed. Michael Holquist, trans. Caryl Emerson and Michael Holquist (Austin: University of Texas Press, 1981), 75.

236 Ibiwari Ikiriko, *Oily Tears of the Delta* (Ibadan: Kraft Books Limited, 2000), 11.

237 Ikiriko, 11–12.

238 Ikiriko, 13.

239 Bakhtin, *Dialogic Imagination,* xvii.

240 Ikiriko, 51.

241 Ikiriko, 51.

242 Ikiriko, 51.

243 Bassey, *To Cook a Continent,* 12.

244 Eagleton, *How to Read a Poem,* 21.

245 Ikiriko, 56.

246 Ikiriko, 43.

247 Okunoye, "Alterity", 418.

248 Huggan, 704.

249 Ikiriko, 20.

250 Ikiriko, 6.

251 Amalgam here refers to the historical creation of Nigeria into a modern principality by colonial Britain in 1914 with the amalgamation of Southern and Northern Protectorates into a unified colonial realm.

252 See Franco Moretti, *Atlas of the European Novel* (London: Verso, 1998).

253 Ikiriko, 44.

254 Watts, "Resource Curse?", 50.

255 Quoted in Sule Egya, "Imagining Beast: Images of the Oppressor in Recent Nigerian Poetry in English", *Journal of Commonwealth Literature*, vol. 46, no. 2 (2011): 350.

256 Amitav Ghosh, "Petrofiction: The Oil Encounter and the Novel". *The Imam and the Indian: Prose Pieces* (New Delhi: Ravi Dayal Publisher, 2002), 79. Reprinted.

257 Nixon, 19.

258 Martin Luther King, Jnr. "Beyond Vietnam: A Time to Break Silence". Speech delivered at a meeting of concerned clergy and laity at Riverside Church in New York City. 4 April 1967.

259 Nixon, 2–10.

260 Jonathan Haynes, "Nnebue: The Anatomy of Power", *Film International*, vol. 5, no. 4, (2007): 32.

261 See Hannah Arendt's *On Violence* (New York: Harcourt Brace, 1969). However, I do not address her views here in relation to Fanon because that has been adequately dealt with in Elizabeth Frazer and Kimberly Hutchings's "On Politics and Violence: Arendt Contra Fanon", *Contemporary Political Theory*, 7 (2008): 90–108. Arguing in defence of Fanon, Frazer and Hutchings write that "violence for freedom, then, goes beyond the straightforward means to an independently conceived end. Rather, it is thought as the expression of human freedom" (91); one that Jean-Paul Sartre in the preface to Fanon's *Wretched of the Earth* describes as a process of self-recreation from a condition of enslavement (22).

262 Achille Mbembe, "Reading Fanon in the Twenty-first Century", W.E.B. DuBois Memorial Lecture, Colgate University, New York, 15 November 2010.

263 Itse Sagay, "Nigeria: Federalism, the Constitution and Resource Control". *Urhobo Historical Society*. 19 May 2001. www.waado.org/nigerdelta/essays/resourcecontrol/HomePage.html

264 Jean-Paul Sartre, "Preface" to *Wretched of the Earth*, 7–31.

265 Sartre, 21.

266 Nixon, 3–6.

267 Nixon, 7.

268 For a comprehensive study of the evolution and practices of the Nigerian film industry, see Hyginus Ekwuazi, *Film in Nigeria* (Jos: Nigerian Film Corporation, 1991); Onookome Okome, "Nollywood and Its Critics", in *Viewing African Cinema in the Twenty-First Century: Art Films and the Nollywood Video Revolution*, eds. Mahir Saul and Ralph A. Austen. (Athens: Ohio University Press, 2010), 26–41.

269 Okome, "Nollywood and Its Critics, 146.

270 Chukwuma Okoye, "Looking at Ourselves in our Mirror: Agency, Counter-Discourse, and the Nigerian Video Film", *Film International*, vol. 5, no. 4 (2007), 26.

271 See, for instance, films such as *The Liquid Black Gold* (dir. Ikenna Aniekwe, 2010), *Crude War* (written by Ikenna Aniekwe and dir. Ugezu J. Ugezu, 2010), and *The Amnesty* (Screenplay/dir. Ikenna Aniekwe, 2011). There is a sense of strategic astuteness about these artists in their representation of violence and the geopolitics that stoke it in the Delta. In the film under analysis, we encounter the way they surface certain elided instances of the oil encounter, where cultures are displaced, cultural links severed, kinship ties fractioned, basic human weaknesses exploited, and nonsense is made of local heroes and heroines.

272 Hope Eghagha, "Magical Realism and the 'Power' of Nollywood Home Video Films", *Film International*, vol. 5, no. 4 (2007), 74.

273 Onookome Okome, "Nollywood: Africa at the Movies" *Film International*, vol. 5, no. 4 (2007), 4.

274 Ukata, 6.

275 Bakhtin, *Dialogic Imagination*, 75.

276 Alison Levine, "Words on Trial: Oral Performance in Abderrahamane Sissako's Bamako", *Studies in French Cinema*, vol. 22, no. 2 (2012): 151–167.

277 Walter Benjamin, "The Story-Teller: Reflections on the Works of Nicolai Leskov", *Chicago Review*, vol. 16, no. 1 (1963): 80–101.

278 Benjamin, 83.

279 Benjamin, 85–86.

280 Benjamin, 87.

281 Benjamin, 87.

282 Benjamin, 95.

283 Benjamin, 95.

284 Tejumola Olaniyan, "Narrativizing Postcoloniality: Responsibilities", *Public Cultures*, vol. 5, no. 1 (1992): 51.

285 The trajectory of oil in the Delta can be followed to arrive at an understanding of the spectacle of violence as evidenced in the region, and an apparently discordant feature of politics that built up to the present in Nigeria. This video film draws heavily from the debates that emanate from the discourses of resource control and principles of derivation that have underscored Nigeria's history since independence.

286 In the introductory chapter of this book, I briefly discussed the historical contexts in which Saro-Wiwa championed the Niger Delta struggle. What I left out is a bitter generational and ideological rivalry between him (Saro-Wiwa) and his one-time mentor and subsequent political rival, Chief Edward Kobani, in the Ogoni saga. This rivalry, it is argued, brought about mistrust, resulting in the mobbing of four Ogoni Elders in 1994 by some irate Ogoni youths. It was for this (unsubstantiated) reason that Saro-Wiwa was tried and hanged in 1995 by the Abacha junta. Adewale Meja-Pearce has a more detailed discussion of this angle to the Ogoni struggle in his book of essays, *Remembering Ken Saro-Wiwa and Other Essays*, especially pages 9–48.

287 Fanon, 148–205.

288 See Obi and Rustad (2011).

289 Abiodun Alao, *Natural Resources and Conflict in Africa: The Tragedy of Endowment* (New York: University of Rochester Press, 2007), x.

290 See the Willink Commission of 1958 set up to address the fears of minorities and the means of allaying them; the Oil Mineral Producing Area Development Commission (OMPADEC) of 1992; the Niger Delta Development Commission of 2000; and more recently, the Amnesty Disarmament Commission, which later mutated into the Federal Ministry of the Niger Delta in 2009.

291 Obi and Rustad, 2.

292 See Ikelegbe, and Ukiwo, in Obi and Rustad, eds. (2011).

293 Alabi Williams, "Interview with Nnimmo Bassey", Sunday Special Report: The Niger Delta. *The Nigerian Guardian*, 13 July 2008.

294 Obi and Rustad, 3.

295 Ferguson, 201.

296 Ferguson, 205.

297 Timothy Hunt, *Politics of Bones: Dr Owens Wiwa and the Struggle for Nigeria's Oil* (Toronto: McClelland & Stewart, 2006), 96–97.

298 Fanon, 51.

299 Slavoj Zizek, *Violence: Six Sideways Reflections* (New York: Picador, 2008), 12. (Italics added for emphasis.)

300 Imre Szeman, "Crude Aesthetics: The Politics of Oil Documentaries", *Journal of American Studies*, vol. 46, no. 2 (2012): 432.

301 Noel Carroll, "Narrative Closure", *Philos Stud*, vol. 135 (2007): 1–15.

302 Philip Aghoghovwia, "Review of Fragments from the History of Loss: the Nature Industry and the Postcolony", *Social Dynamics* (2022): 2. Retrieved from: https://doi.org/10.1080/0253 3952.2022.2022258

303 Zina Saro-Wiwa, dir., 2015. "Karikpo Pipeline", 5-channel digital video, 27 mins 31 secs. http://www.zinasarowiwa.com/video/karikpo/.

304 Z. Saro-Wiwa, "Karikpo Pipeline".

305 See Eghosa Osaghae (1995); Okome, *Before I am Hanged* (2000); Obi and Rustad (2011); and Michael Ross, *The Oil Curse* (Princeton: Princeton University Press, 2012).

306 Dipesh Chakrabarty, "Postcolonial Studies and the Challenge of Climate Change", *New Literary History*, vol. 43, no. 1 (2012): 1.

307 Achille Mbembe, "At the Edge of the World: Boundaries, Territoriality, and Sovereignty in Africa", *Public Culture*, vol. 12, no. 1 (2000): 260.

308 Mbembe, 284.

309 Morton, *Hyperobject*, 1.

310 Ken Saro-Wiwa, *A Month and a Day: A Detention Dairy* (London: Penguin, 1995), 126.

311 LeMenager, "Eden if We Dare", 39.

312 LeMenager, 45.

References

Adesanmi, Pius and Chris Dunton. "Nigeria's Third Generation Writing: Historiography and Preliminary Theoretical Considerations". *English in Africa*, vol. 32, no. 1, 2005, pp. 7–19

Agambem, Giogio. *Homo Sacer: Sovereign Power and Bare Life*, translated by Daniel Heller Roazen. Stanford University Press, 1998

Aghoghovwia, Philip. "Review of Fragments from the History of Loss: The Nature Industry and the Postcolony". *Social Dynamics*, vol. 48, no. 1, 2022, pp. 184–189. Retrieved from: https://doi.org/10.1080/02533952.2022.2022258

Aghoghovwia, Philip. "Is the Anthropocene Conniving with Capital? Water Priva(tisa)tion and Ontology Reimagined in Karen Jayes' *For the Mercy of Water*". *Interventions*, vol. 24, no. 3, 2022, pp. 434–450. Retrieved from: https://doi.org/10.1080/1369801X.2021.2015704

Aghoghovwia, Philip. "Anthropocene Arts: Apocalyptic Realism and the Post-Oil Omaginary in the Niger Delta", in *Climate Realism: The Aesthetics of Weather and Atmosphere in the Anthropcene,* edited by Lynn Badia, Marija Cetinic and Jeff Diamanti. Routledge, 2020, pp. 33–46

Aghoghovwia, Philip. "Poetics of Cartography: Globalism and the 'Oil Enclave' in Ibiwari Ikiriko's *Oily Tears of the Delta*". *Social Dynamics*, vol. 43, no. 1, 2017, pp. 32–45

Aghoghovwia, Philip. "Postcolonial Nature", in *Nature and Literary Studies,* edited by Peter Remien and Scott Slovic. Cambridge University Press, 2022, pp. 211-228.

Aiyejina, Funsho. "Recent Nigerian Poetry in English: An Alter/native Tradition", in *Perspectives on Nigerian Literature 1700 to the Present*, Guardian Publishing, 1988, p. 124

Alao, Abiodun. *Natural Resources and Conflict in Africa: The Tragedy of Endowment.* University of Rochester Press, 2007

Altvater, Elmar. "The Capitalocene, or, Geoengineering against Capitalism's Planetary Boundaries", in *Anthropocene or Capitalocene? Nature, History, and the Crisis of Capitalism,* edited by Jason Moore. Kairos, 2016, pp. 138–152

Amnesty International. *Bad Information: Oil Spill Investigations in the Niger Delta. Amnesty International Publications*, 2013. Retrieved from: https://www.amnesty.org/en/documents/afr44/028/2013/en/

Anderson, Hilary. "Hundreds of People Burned to Death in Southern Nigeria". BBC Online News Report. Warri: British Broadcasting Corporation, 19 October 1998

Anderson, Paul T., dir. *There Will Be Blood*. Perf. Daniel Day-Lewis and Paul Dano. 2007. DVD

Aniekwe, Ikenna, dir. *The Liquid Black Gold*. Perf. Justus Esiri, Enebeli Elebuwa, Sam Dede, and Gentle Jack. Ossy Affasson Limited, 2010. DVD

Apter, Andrew H. *The Pan-African Nation: Oil and the Spectacle of Culture in Nigeria.* University of Chicago Press, 2005

Arendt, Hannah. *On Violence.* Harcourt Brace, 1969

Awhefeada, Sunny. "Degraded Environment and Destabilized Women in Kaine Agary's Yellow-

Yellow", in *Eco-Critical Literature: Regreening African Landscapes*, edited by Ogaga Okuyade. African Heritage Press, 2013, pp. 95–108

Awhefeada, Sunny. "History and the Politics of Representation in the Postcolonial African Text", in *Politics of the Postcolonial Text,* edited by James Tsaaior. Lincom Europa, 2010, pp. 172–187

Ayobade, Oladotun. "Women that Danced the Fire Dance: Fela Kuti's Afrobeat Queens, Performance and the Dialectics of Postcolonial Identity". Unpublished PhD Diss., University of Texas at Austin, 2016

Bachelard, Gaston. *The Psychoanalysis of Fire*. Routledge, 1964

Baird, Vanessa. "Arts: The Bard of Environmental Justice Speaks". *New Internationalist* (2011), pp. 39–40

Bakhtin, Mikhail. *Speech Genres & Other Late Essays*, edited by Caryl Emerson and Michael Holsquist. University of Texas Press, 2004

Bakhtin, Mikhail. *The Bakhtin Reader: Selected Writings of Bakhtin*, edited by Medvedev and Voloshinov. Arnold Publishers, 1994

Bakhtin, Mikhail. "Literary Stylistics: The Construction of the Utterance", in *Bakhtin School Papers*, translated by Noel Owen. Oxford University Press, 1987, pp. 114–115

Bakhtin, Mikhail. *Rabelais and His World,* translated by Helene Iswolsky. Indiana University Press, 1984

Bakhtin, Mikhail. *The Dialogic Imagination: Four Essays,* edited by Michael Holquist, translated by Caryl Emerson and Michael Holquist. University of Texas Press, 1981

Bassey, Nnimmo. *To Cook a Continent: Destructive Extraction and the Climate Crisis in Africa*. Pambazuka Press, 2012

Bassey, Nnimmo. "A Movement is Not a Bicycle Wheel". Speech delivered at a Town Hall Meeting on Fracking and Shell Petroleum Company, Liberty Hall Theatre, Dublin, 21 June 2012

Bassey, Nnimmo. "Leave it in the Ground". *New Internationalist*, vol. 419, no. 1, 2009 Retrieved from: https://newint.org/features/2009/01/01/climate-justice-bassey-evans

Bassey, Nnimmo. *We Thought It Was Oil But It Was Blood*. Kraftgriots, 2002

Benjamin, Walter. "The Story-Teller: Reflections on the Works of Nicolai Leskov". *Chicago Review*, vol. 16, no. 1, 1963, pp. 80–101

Bodunde, Charles. "Tanure Ojaide's Poetry and the Delta Landscape: A Study of *Delta Blues and Home Songs*", in *Writing the Homeland: The Poetry and Politics of Tanure Ojaide*, edited by Onookome Okome. Bayreuth African Studies, 2002, p. 201

Bond, Patrick. *Politics of Climate Justice: Paralysis Above, Movement Below*. University of KwaZulu-Natal Press, 2012

Burgis, Tom. *The Looting Machine*. William Collins, 2016

Butler, Judith. *Precarious Life: The Power of Mourning and Violence*. Verso, 2004

Butler, Judith. *Gender Trouble: Feminism and the Subversion of Identity*. Routledge, 1990

Caminero-Santangelo, Byron. *Different Shades of Green: African Literature, Environmental Justice and Political Ecology*. University of Virginia Press, 2014

Carroll, Noel. "Narrative Closure". *Philos Stud*, vol. 135, 2007, pp. 1–15

Chakrabarty, Dipesh. "Anthropocene 1", in *Fuelling Culture: 101 Words for Energy and Environment*, edited by Imre Szeman, Jennifer Wenzel and Patricia Yaeger. Fordham University Press, 2017, pp. 39–42

Chakrabarty, Dipesh. "History on an Expanded Canvas: The Anthropocene's Invitation". Keynote speech presented at The Anthropocene Project: An Opening, Haus der Kulturen de Welt, Berlin, 13 January 2013. Retrieved from: https://youtu.be/svgqLPFpaOg

Chakrabarty, Dipesh. "Postcolonial Studies and the Challenge of Climate Change". *New Literary History*, vol. 43, no. 1, 2012, pp. 1–18

Chakrabarty, Dipesh. "Where is the Now?". *Critical Inquiry*, vol. 30, no. 2, 2004, pp. 458–462

Chinweizu, Onwuchewka Jemie, and Ihechukwu Madubuike. *Toward the Decolonization of African literature*. Vol. 1: *African Fiction and Poetry and Their Critics*. Fourth Dimension Publishers, 1980

Chomsky, Noam. "The Anthropocene, 6th Extinction, and Climate Change". Lecture presented at St Olaf College, USA, 6 May 2018. Retrieved from: https://youtu.be/kjIsuGHdbnw

Clark, John Pepper. *The Raft*, Oxford University Press, 1964

Cohen, Jeffrey and Lowell Duckert. "Introduction: Eleven Principles of the Elements", in *Elemental Ecocriticism: Thinking with Earth, Air, Water and Fire*, edited by Jeffrey Cohen and Lowell Duckert. University of Minnesota Press, 2015, pp. 1–26

Crist, Eileen. "On the Poverty of Our Nomenclature", in *Anthropocene or Capitalocene? Nature, History, and the Crisis of Capitalism*, edited by Jason Moore. Kairos, 2016, pp. 14–33

Crutzen, Paul and Eugene Stoermer. "The Anthropocene". *IGPB (International Geosphere-Biosphere Programme) Newsletter*, no. 41 (2000), pp. 17–18

Crutzen, Paul. "Geology of Mankind: The Anthropocene". *Nature*, vol. 415, 2002, pp. 22–23

Crutzen, Paul and Will Steffen. "How Long Have We Been in the Anthropocene Era?". *Climate Change*, vol. 63, no. 3, 2003, pp. 251–257

Darah, Godini G. "Revolutionary Pressures in Niger Delta Literatures", in *From Boom to Doom: Protest and Conflict Resolutions in the Literature of the Niger Delta*, edited by Chinyere Nwahunanya. Springfield Publishers, 2011, pp. 1–22

Democracy Now: A Daily Independent TV/Radio Global News Hour Program with Amy Goodman and Juan Gonzalez. Rio de Janeiro, Thursday, 21 June 2012. Retrieved from: http://www.democracynow.org

Eagleton, Terry. *How to Read a Poem*. Blackwell Publishing, 2007.

Eghagha, Hope. "Magical Realism and the 'Power' of Nollywood Home Video Films". *Film International*, vol. 5, no. 4, 2007, p. 74

Egya, Sule. "Literary Militancy and Helon Habila's Oil on Water". *Research in African Literatures*, vol. 48, no. 4, 2017, pp. 94–104

Egya, Sule. *Nation, Power and Dissidence in Third-Generation Nigerian Poetry in English*. UNISA Press, 2014

Egya, Sule. "Eco-Human Engagement in Recent Nigerian Poetry in English". *Journal of Postcolonial Writing*, vol. 49, no. 1, 2013, pp. 60–70

Egya, Sule. "Imagining Beast: Images of the Oppressor in Recent Nigerian Poetry in English".

Journal of Commonwealth Literature, vol. 46, no. 2, 2011, p. 345–358

Ekwuazi, Hyginus. *Film in Nigeria*. Nigerian Film Corporation, 1991

Fanon, Frantz. *The Wretched of the Earth*. Penguin, 1961

Feghabo, Charles. "Inverting Otherness in Kaine Agary's Yellow-Yellow". *Matatu*, vol. 45, 2014, pp. 315–332

Ferguson, James. *Global Shadows: Africa in the Neoliberal World Order,* Duke University Press, 2006

Frazer, Elizabeth and Kimberly Hutchings. "On Politics and Violence: Arendt Contra Fanon". *Contemporary Political Theory*, vol. 7, 2008, pp. 90–108

Frye, Northrop. "Preface", in *The Psychoanalysis of Fire*, by Gaston Bachelard. Routledge, 1964, pp. v–viii

Fulford, Robert. *The Triumph of the Narrative*. Anansi, 1999

Garrard, Greg. *Ecocriticism: The New Critical Idiom*. Routledge, 2004

Garuba, Harry. "The Unbearable Lightness of Being: Re-figuring Trends in Recent Nigerian Poetry", *English in Africa*, vol. 32, no. 1, 2005, pp. 51–72

Garuba, Harry. "Ken Saro-Wiwa's Sozaboy and the Logic of Minority Discourse", in *Ogoni Agonies: Ken Saro-Wiwa and the Crises in Nigeria,* edited by Abdul-Rasheed Na-Allah. Africa World Press, 1998, pp. 229–239

Ghosh, Amitav. *The Great Derangement: Climate Change and the Unthinkable*. University of Chicago Press, 2016

Ghosh, Amitav. "Petrofiction: The Oil Encounter and the Novel", in *The Imam and the Indian: Prose Pieces*. Ravi Dayal Publisher, 2002, pp. 75–89

Goldberg, David T. "Epistemologies of Deception: Topologies of the Extra/Ordinary". *The Johannesburg Salon*, vol. 5, 2012, pp. 51–62

Green, Louise. *Fragments from the History of Loss: The Nature Industry and the Postcolony*. Pennsylvania State University Press, 2020

Green, Louise. "The Aphorism and the Historical Image: Adorno's Politics of Form". *The Johannesburg Salon*, vol. 5, 2012, pp. 80 –85

Guha, Ramachandra and Juan Martinez-Alier. *Varieties of Environmentalism: Essays North and South*. Earthscan, 1997

Harris, Anne. "Pyromena Fire's Doing". *Elemental Ecocriticism: Thinking with Earth, Air, Water and Fire,* edited by Jeffrey Cohen and Lowell Duckert. University of Minnesota Press, 2015, pp. 27–54

Haynes, Jonathan. "Nnebue: The Anatomy of Power". *Film International*, vol. 5, no. 4, 2007, pp. 30–37

Huggan, Graham and Helen Tiffin. *Postcolonial Ecocriticism: Literature, Animals, Environment*. Routledge, 2010

Huggan, Graham. "'Greening' Postcolonialism: Ecocritical Perspectives". *Modern Fiction Studies*, vol. 50, no. 3, 2004, pp. 701–733

Hunt, Timothy. *Politics of Bones: Dr Owens Wiwa and the Struggle for Nigeria's Oil*. McClelland &

Stewart, 2006

Ifowodo, Ogaga. *The Oil Lamp*. Africa World Press, 2005

Iheka, Cajetan. *Naturalizing Africa: Ecological Violence, Agency, and Postcolonial Resistance in African Literature*. Cambridge University Press, 2018

Ikiriko, Ibiwari. *Oily Tears of the Delta*. Kraft Books, 2000

Jupiter, Tony. "The Jesse Fire Disaster". BBC Online News. Warri: British Broadcasting Corporation, 19 October 1998

Kaze, Douglas. "The Environmental Imagination in Arthur Nortje's Poetry". Unpublished PhD Diss., Rhodes University, 2018

King, Martin Luther, Jnr. "Beyond Vietnam: A Time to Break Silence". Speech delivered at a meeting of concerned clergy and laity at Riverside Church in New York City, 4 April 1967

Klein, Naomi. "Let Them Drown: The Violence of Othering in a Warming World". *London Review of Books*, vol. 38, no. 11, 2016, pp. 11–14

Klein, Naomi. *This Changes Everything: Capitalism vs The Climate*. Simon & Schuster, 2014

LeMenager, Stephanie. "Eden If We Dare", in *Did You Know We Taught Them How to Dance?*. Blaffer Art Museum, University of Houston, 2016, pp. 39–45

Levine, Alison. "Words on Trial: Oral Performance in Abderrahamane Sissako's Bamako". *Studies in French Cinema*, vol. 22, no. 2, 2012, pp. 151–167

Martin, Pamela L. "Global Governance from the Amazon: Leaving Oil Underground in Yasuni National Park, Ecuador". *Global Environmental Politics*, vol. 11, no. 4, 2011, pp. 22–42

Mbembe, Achille. "Footnotes on the Offshore City". *The Johannesburg Salon*, vol. 7, 2014, pp. 142–143

Mbembe, Achille. "Reading Fanon in the Twenty-first Century". W.E.B. DuBois Memorial Lecture. Colgate University, 15 November 2010

Mbembe, Achille . "At the Edge of the World: Boundaries, Territoriality, and Sovereignty in Africa". *Public Culture*, vol. 12, no. 1, 2000, pp. 259–284

Meja-Pearce, Adewale. "Feed the Charm: Review of *In the Shadow of a Saint: A Son's Journey to Understand His Father's Legacy* by Ken Wiwa". *London Review of Books*, vol. 24, no. 14, 2002, pp. 23–26

Meja-Pearce, Adewale. *Remembering Ken Saro-Wiwa and Other Essays*. The New Gong, 2005

Mitchell, Timothy. "Carbon Democracy". *Economy and Society*, vol. 38, no. 3, 2009, pp. 399–432

Moore, Jason. ed. *Anthropocene or Capitalocene? Nature, History, and the Crisis of Capitalism*. Kairos, 2016

Moretti, Franko. *Atlas of the European Novel*. Verso Books, 1998

Morrison, Toni. "The Site of Memory", in *Inventing the Truth: The Art and Craft of Memoir*, edited by William Zinsser, 2nd edition. Houghton Mifflin, 1995, pp. 83–102

Mortimer, Mildred. *Writing from the Hearth: Public, Domestic and Imaginative Space in Francophone Women's Fiction of Africa and the Caribbean*. Lexington Books, 2007

Morton, Timothy. *Hyperobjects: Philosophy and Ecology After the End of the World*. University of Minnesota Press, 2013

Morton, Timothy . *The Ecological Thought*. Harvard University Press, 2010

Mukherjee, Pablo. *Postcolonial Environments, Nature, Culture and the Contemporary Indian Novel in English*. Palgrave, 2010

Newell, Stephanie. *West African Literatures: Ways of Reading*. Oxford University Press, 2006

Nixon, Rob. "Anthropocene 2", in *Fuelling Culture: 101 Words for Energy and Environment*, edited by Imre Szeman, Jennifer Wenzel and Patricia Yaeger. Fordham University Press, 2017, pp. 43–46

Nixon, Rob. *Slow Violence and the Environmentalism of the Poor*, Harvard University Press, 2011

Nkosi, Lewis. *Tasks and Masks: Themes and Styles of African Literature*, Longman, 1981

Nnamdi, Basil, Obari Gomba and Frank Ugiomoh. "Environmental Challenges and Eco-Aesthetics in Nigeria's Niger Delta". *Third Text*, vol. 27, no. 1, 2013, pp. 65–75

Nwagbara, Uzoechi. "Poetics of Resistance: Ecocitical Reading of Ojaide's Delta Blues and Daydream of Ants". *African Study Monographs*, vol. 31, no. 1, 2010, p. 17

Nwahunanya, Chinyere. "Introduction: From Boom to Doom – The Niger Delta in Contemporary Nigerian Literature", in *From Boom to Doom: Protest and Conflict Resolutions in the Literature of the Niger Delta*, edited by Chinyere Nwahunanya. Springfield Publishers, 2011, pp. iv–xxi

Obi, Cyril and Siri Rustad. Eds. *Oil and Insurgency in the Niger Delta*. Nordic Africa Institute, 2011

Obiechina, Emmanuel. "Poetry as Therapy: Reflections on Achebe's "Christmas in Biafra" and Other Poems". *Callaloo*, vol. 25, no. 2, 2002, pp. 527–558

Ojaide, Tanure and Enajite Ojaruega. Eds. *The Literature and Arts of the Niger Delta*. Routledge, 2021

Ojaide, Tanure. *Delta Blues & Home Songs*. Kraft Books, 1998

Ojaide, Tanure . "I Want to Be an Oracle: My Poetry and My Generation". *World Literature Today*, vol. 68, no. 1, 1994, pp. 15–21

Okome, Onookome. "Nollywood and Its Critics", in *Viewing African Cinema in the Twenty-First Century: Art Films and the Nollywood Video Revolution*, edited by Mahir Saul and Ralph Austen. Ohio University Press, 2010, pp. 26–41

Okome, Onookome. "Nollywood: Africa at the Movies". *Film International*, vol. 5, no. 4, 2007, p. 4

Okome, Onookome. Ed. *Before I Am Hanged: Ken Saro-Wiwa; Literature, Politics and Dissent*. Africa World Press, 2000

Okonta Ike, and Oronto Douglas, *Where Vultures Feast: Shell, Human Rights and Oil in the Niger Delta*. Verso Books, 2003

Okoye, Chukwuma. "Looking at Ourselves in Our Mirror: Agency, Counter-Discourse and the Nigerian Video Film". *Film International*, vol. 5, no. 4, 2007, p. 26

Okunoye, Oyeniyi. "Alterity, Marginality and the National Question in the Poetry of the Niger Delta". *Cahiers d' Etudes Africaines*, vol. 191, no. 3, 2008, pp. 413–436

Okunoye, Oyeniyi. "Writing Resistance: Dissidence and Visions of Healing in Nigerian Poetry of the Military Era". *Tydskrif vir Letterkunde*, vol. 48, no. 1, 2011, pp. 64–85

Okuyade, Ogaga. "The Cumulative Neglect of Collective Responsibility: Postcoloniality, Ecology and the Niger Delta". *Matatu*, vol. 39, no. 7, 2011, pp. 115–131

Olaniyan, Tejumola. "Narrativizing Postcoloniality: Responsibilities". *Public Cultures*, vol. 5, no. 1, 1992, pp. 47–55

Olaoluwa, Senayon. "Dislocating Anthropocene: The City and Oil in Helon Habila's *Oil on Water*". *ISLE: Interdisciplinary Studies in Literature and Environment,* vol. 27, no. 2, 2020, pp. 243–267

Osaghae, Eghosa. "The Ogoni Uprising". *African Affairs,* vol. 95, 1995, pp. 325–344

Osundare, Niyi. *Dialogue with My Country.* Bookcraft, 2007

Otiono, Nduka. "Saro-Wiwa's Ghost: The Niger Delta Struggle and Nollywood Filmic Representation". *Petrocultures: Oil, Energy, Cultures Conference.* University of Alberta, Canada, 9 September 2012

Parini, Jay. *Why Poetry Matters.* Yale University Press, 2008

Pilkington, Ed. "Shell Pays Out $15.5m over Saro-Wiwa Killing". *The Guardian*, Tuesday, 9 June 2009: Retrieved from: http://www.guardian.co.uk/world/2009/jun/08/nigeria-usa

Plumwood, Val. *Environmental Culture: The Ecological Crisis of Reason.* Routledge, 2001

Quayson, Ato. *Calibrations: Reading for the Social.* University of Minnesota Press, 2003

Ross, Michael. *The Oil Curse.* Princeton University Press, 2012

Sagay, Itse. "Nigeria: Federalism, the Constitution and Resource Control". *Urhobo Historical Society.* 19 May 2001. Retreived from http://www.waado.org/nigerdelta/essays/resourcecontrol/HomePage.html

Sallah, Tijan. "The Eagle's Vision: The Poetry of Tanure Ojaide". *Research in African Literatures,* vol. 26, no. 1, 1995, p. 21

Said, Edward. "Opponents, Audiences, Constituencies, and Community". *Critical Inquiry,* vol. 9, no. 1, 1982, pp. 1–26

Saro-Wiwa, Ken. *Genocide in Nigeria: The Ogoni Tragedy.* Saros International, 1992

Saro-Wiwa, Zina. "Karikpo Pipeline (2015) 5-channel video installation 27mins 31secs". Zina Saro Wiwa (website). Retrieved from: http://www.zinasarowiwa.com/video/karikpo/

Sartre, Jean-Paul. "Preface" to *Wretched of the Earth*, by Frantz Fanon. Penguin, 1961, pp. 7–26

Sinclair, Upton. *Oil!.* Penguin, 2007

Stavans, Ilan. "Is American Literature Parochial?". *World Literature Today*, vol. 87, no. 4, 2013, pp. 26–30

Steffen, Will. "The Anthropocene". Filmed 4 November 2010, in Canberra, Australia. TEDx video, 18:15. Retrieved from: https://youtu.be/ABZjlfhN0EQ

Steffen, Will. "The Anthropocene: Where on Earth Are We Going?". Keynote speech presented at The Anthropocene Project: An Opening, Haus der Kulturen der Welt, Berlin, January 10, 2013. Retrieved from: https://youtu.be/T8U6y4UNXRQ

Stelzig, Christine, Eva Ursprung and Stefan Eisenhofer. Eds. *Last Rites Niger Delta: The Drama of Oil Production in Contemporary Photographs,* Staatliches Museum fur Volkerkunde Munchen, 2012

Szeman, Imre. "Crude Aesthetics: The Politics of Oil Documentaries". *Journal of American Studies*, vol. 46, no. 2, 2012, pp. 423–439

Temper, Leah, Ivonne Yanez, Khadija Sharife, Godwin Ojo and Joan Martinez-Alier. *Towards a Post-Oil Civilization: Yasunization and Other Initiatives to Leave Fossil Fuels in the Soil.* EJOLT Report no. 6, 2013, p. 6

Tsaaior, James. "Poetics, Politics and the Paradoxes of Oil in Nigeria's Niger Delta Region". *African Renaissance,* vol. 2, no. 6, 2005, pp. 72–80

Ukata, Agatha. "Images of Women in Nigerian (Nollywood) Videos". Unpublished PhD thesis, University of the Witwatersrand, 2010

United Nations Environment Programme. *Environmental Assessment of Ogoniland Report,* 2011. Retrieved from: https://www.unep.org/explore-topics/disasters-conflicts/where-we-work/nigeria/environmental-assessment-ogoniland-report.

Vieira, Fátima. "The Concept of Utopia". *The Cambridge Companion to Utopian Literature*, edited by Gregory Claeys. Cambridge University Press, 2010

Watts, Michael. "Blood Oil: The Anatomy of a Petro-Insurgency in the Niger Delta, Nigeria", in *Crude Domination: An Anthology of Oil,* edited by Andrea Berhrends and Stephen P Reyna. Berghan Books, 2011, pp. 49–80

Watts, Michael. "Petro-Insurgency or Criminal Syndicate?". *Review of African Political Economy,* vol. 114, 2007, pp. 637–660

Watts, Michael. "Resource Curse? Governmentality, Oil and Power in the Niger Delta, Nigeria", *Geopolitics*, vol. 9, no. 1, 2004, pp. 50–80

Wenzel, Jennifer. *The Disposition of Nature: Environmental Crisis and World Literature.* Fordham University Press, 2020

Wheen, Francis. *How Mumbo-Jumbo Conquered the World.* Harper Perennial, 2004

Williams, Alabi. "Interview with Nnimmo Bassey", Sunday Special Report: The Niger Delta. *The Nigerian Guardian,* 13 July 2008

Wiwa, Ken. *In the Shadow of a Saint: A Son's Journey to Understand His Father's Legacy.* Penguin Random House Canada, 2000

Yeibo, Ebi. *A Song for Tomorrow.* Kraftgriots, 2003

Zalasiewicz, Jan, Mark Williams, Will Steffen and Paul Crutzen. "The New World of Anthropocene". *Environmental Science & Technology,* vol. 44, no. 7, 2010, pp. 2228–2231

Zizek, Slavoj. *Violence: Six Sideways Reflections.* Picador, 2008

Index